Holton, William C.

Cruise of the U.S. flag-ship Hartford 1862-1863

Inktank publishing

Holton, William C.

Cruise of the U.S. flag-ship Hartford 1862-1863

Inktank publishing, 2018

www.inktank-publishing.com

ISBN/EAN: 9783747775264

CRUISE

OF THE

U. S. FLAG-SHIP HARTFORD,

1862--1863:

BEING

A NARRATIVE OF ALL HER OPERATIONS SINCE GOING INTO COMMISSION, IN 1862, UNTIL HER RETURN TO NEW YORK IN 1863.

FROM THE PRIVATE JOURNAL OF WILLIAM C. HOLTON.

BY B. S. OSBON.

NEW YORK
L. W. PAINE, PRINTER, No. 37 PARK ROW
1863.

THE HARTFORD AS A TRAINING SHIP

To the Editor of the New York Times:

The Board of Education has asked the Navy Department to loan the City of New York the historic old flag-ship Hartford, to take the place of the sailing sloop-of-war St. Mary's, which for over thirty years has done such good service at this port as a nautical school-ship for the merchant marine.

The St. Mary's is by far too small to accommodate the increasing demand for admission to the school. In the age of steam and electricity, too, she is not up to the standard of requirements for such an institution. The Hartford is the most suitable vessel that seems to be available at the present time, and could accommodate over 300 pupils and the necessary staff of officers and a crew of able seamen.

It is rumored that there is some objection at Washington to transferring the Hartford to this city, probably on sentimental grounds, and instead to loan the gunboat Topeka, a most unsuitable vessel for the school, for she is schooner-rigged—a coal-consuming craft that would entail a needless expense upon the board.

After all the Board of Education has done for the navy and merchant marine of this country by turning out so many clever men for both services, it should be the pleasure as well as the duty of the department to loan the Hartford, which would be kept in excellent condition and ready for any emergency.

B. S. Osbon.

(Farragut's Fleet Signal Officer in 1862.)

New York, May 3, 1906.

PREFACE

WHEN this journal was commenced, and until within a few days since, no idea of its publication was entertained, and it has been forced into type only by the earnest solicitation of the officers and crew of the noble ship which has been our home for nearly two years. The anxiety of our friends has led us to push the completion of this little book to as speedy a close as possible; therefore our readers must not look for any display of literary attainments, but receive it as a correct epitome of our cruise on the Mississippi.

W. C. H.

JOURNAL OF THE CRUISE OF THE "HARTFORD"

JOURNAL OF THE CRUISE

OF THE

FLAG-SHIP HARTFORD.

U. S. FLAG-SHIP HARTFORD,
Philadelphia, Jan. 19, 1862.

HIS morning, at 10 o'clock, the U. S. screw sloop *Hartford* was put in commission as the flag-ship of the Western Gulf Blockading Squadron. The following is a list of officers ordered to join her:

Flag Officer—DAVID G. FARRAGUT.
Fleet Captain—HENRY H. BELL.
Commander—RICHARD WAINWRIGHT.
Lieutenant and Executive Officer—JAS. S. THORNTON.
Lieutenant and Ordnance Officer—ALBERT KAUTZ.
Surgeon—W. MAXWELL WOOD.
Assistant Surgeon—JOSEPH HUGG.
Paymaster—GEORGE PLUNKETT.
Master—JOHN C. WATSON.
Acting Masters—D. S. MURPHY, C. DESAMES, JOS. G. LEWIS.
Marine Officers—1st Lieut., JOHN L. BROOME; 2d Lieut., GEO. HEISLER.
Flag Officer's Secretary—THOMAS WALDEN.
Flag Officer's Clerk—B. S. OSBON.
Acting Midshipmen—H. B. TYSON, E. C. HAZELTINE, JNO. H. REED, H. J. BLAKE.
Engineers—Chief, J. B. KIMBALL; 2d Assistant, JNO. PURDY, E. B. LATCH, F. A. WILSON; 3d Assistant, C. M. BURCHARD, ISAAC DEGRAFF, A. K. FULTON, C. J. COOPER.
Boatswain—JAMES WALKER.
Gunner—JAS. DUNCAN.

Acting Carpenter—J. H. CONLEY.

Acting Sailmaker—JNO. A. HOLBROOK.

Clerks—Captain's, A. D. BACHE; Fleet Captain's, T. B. WADDELL; Paymaster's, F. C. PLUNKETT.

Master's Mates—E. J. ALLEN, THOS. MASON, LEWIS S. LOCKE.

The first business of the crew was to put the ship in sailing order, which, with taking on board provisions and the like, occupied several days. We dropped down to Newcastle, Del. and remained a couple of days, and then went back to Fort Mifflin and took in powder, which is said to be the last article taken on board before sailing, and the first article discharged on returning from a cruise. We then dropped down to Newcastle again, and after receiving on board the Flag Officer and the Fleet Captain, Henry H. Bell, with a salute, proceeded to sea.

On the 28th of January, we sailed for Fortress Monroe, and proceeded down the Delaware, amid a quantity of ice, which was daily increasing. The weather had been stormy for several days, and the men working in the cold rains had in many instances contracted severe lung diseases, so that at the time of sailing there were some fifteen patients in bed and a large number of others under treatment; besides, the ship was in a disordered state, which is always the case with a ship just in commission under such circumstances.

Our ship is a first class steam sloop-of-war, carrying twenty nine-inch Dahlgren guns, besides two twenty-lb. rifled pivots, and a supply of howitzers.

We arrived at Fortress Monroe on the 29th, where we found five men-of-war, three of them American and two French; among them was the U. S. Frigates *Minnesota* and *Roanoke*. We lay there four days, during which time Surgeon Wood was detached and ordered on board the *Minnesota*, with the understanding that we were to find an experienced surgeon on board the frigate *Niagara*, which then lay off Ship Island. We left here on Sunday, February 2d, and stood for Port Royal, and had a middling kind of passage, the weather being somewhat stormy and the ship rolling considerably.

On Tuesday at 3:10 P. M., a man died of measles, and an hour afterwards we reached Port Royal and cast anchor among a fleet of naval vessels. The land here is low and sandy, and covered with trees which to all appearances were the Palmetto. As I looked inland from our anchorage I could see one of the captured forts on our left; but few buildings of any kind were visible; quite a number of Commodore Dupont's fleet were still here, a prominent one being the flag-ship *Wabash*, which had been somewhat damaged in the recent taking of the place.

We left the place on the 6th for Key West, and having a head wind all the way made slight progress, though the weather was pleasant, having lost much of the chilliness of the Delaware region. We arrived at Key West on the 11th February, where we met and were saluted by the U. S. steam sloop of war *Pensacola*; the U. S. steamer *Connecticut* was also here, and the famous yacht *Wanderer*, and several mortar boats of Captain Porter's fleet.

Fort Taylor at this place is quite a formidable looking structure, mounting fifty to seventy-five guns, I should judge, and situated near it is the U. S. Hospital, surrounded with evergreens and quite inviting. The inhabitants are said to number about five thousand. After being at sea this place looks pleasant; cocoa trees spring up here spontaneously, and for a few cents each I obtained a small supply of oranges. We coaled ship here, and sent our letters home by the U. S. steamer *Connecticut*; here we buried another man, an aged fireman; the weather strongly reminded me of hats, and several of the officers laid in a supply for future use.

We left Key West on the 15th for Havana, and had a pleasant passage, arriving there after dark on the same day, a Spanish pilot coming off and taking us into the harbor. The bay in the evening was beautiful in the extreme; there were several large men-of-war in port, of different nations; also a large number of merchantmen. The evening sky was clear as day, and locomotives snorting so naturally reminded one forcibly of home, sweet home.

The day following was Sunday, and it was nearly all spent in exchanging salutes with the English, French and Spanish men-of-war, receiving the U. S. Consul on board with a salute, saluting the Governor, &c. Our war feelings were much excited by seeing two or three Confederate State flags, "the very articles that we were destined to suppress," floating high in the air from the masts of three Confederate merchantmen that were enjoying the protection of this neutral port.

Havana is a pleasant city, situated mostly on a sort of peninsula formed by a pretty bay setting into the land, making a beautiful harbor, with only one narrow and deep outlet which is guarded by the renowned Moro Castle. It is well lighted with gas and supplied with evergreen shade trees, causing a comfortable appearance night or day. Bumboats, so-called, swarm around the ships at anchor, selling oranges, guava jelly, pies and fruit, and articles peculiar to the place and climate.

On the night of the 17th we left this place for Ship Island, to relieve the flag-ship *Niagara*, then stationed there. The weather was pleasant and wind favorable, and we had an agreeable trip. We fell in with schools of the little flying fish which abound in these waters. On the second day out we overhauled and boarded a schooner with the British flag protecting it, though circumstances caused the belief that she was American born at least; on the same afternoon we met and spoke the beautiful new steamship *Constitution*, from Ship Island.

We arrived at Ship Island on the evening of the 20th, received and returned a salute from the frigate *Niagara*, which hauled down her blue pennant on our coming to anchor, thereby transferring her importance to the *Hartford*, and gave us a salute of thirteen guns in honor of our flag-officer, which was duly returned. The *Niagara* had in tow the Confederate steamer *Magnolia*, loaded with eleven hundred bales of cotton, which had been captured on the day previous by the U. S. sloop-of-war *Brooklyn* and the U. S. steamer *South Carolina*, while attempting to run the blockade off the Mississippi.

We here found several U. S. gunboats; among them the *New London* and *Water Witch*, which were scouring the adjacent waters in search of prizes. There were also a few thousand troops on the island, belonging to Brig. Gen. Butler's command. The island is merely a low sand bank, nearly destitute of vegetation, with a little extemporized fort mounting two or three guns, erected, I believe, simply for the present exigencies.

The 21st was signalized by the capture of eleven oyster sloops by the *New London*, which afforded us a taste of the bivalves, which we much enjoyed. On the 22d more prizes arrived, and in the evening the U. S. steam transport *Rhode Island*, loaded with provisions, letters, &c., to gladden the hearts of the sailors and cause a reaction in their monotonous life.

Washington's birth-day was commemorated by salutes from the *Hartford* and *Niagara* and dressing the ships in flags.

February 25th. Had quite a scare through the bursting of one of our boilers, which made a loud report and a large amount of confusion, but did slight damage.

February 27th. Practiced the ship's company at target-firing with the battery; thirty to forty rounds were fired, at some fifteen hundred yards, and some splendid shots were made. The marines were also drilled with muskets at a target.

March 1st. The *Pensacola* arrived from Key West to-day; also a store-ship which brought us two nine-inch guns, increasing our number to twenty-two nine-inch, and two rifled pivots. This morning a boat expedition left the ship in tow of the *New London* for Biloxi, a small village on the main land, and returned in the evening after capturing a few guns and obtaining much valuable information, and without doing any fighting.

March 2d. The *Niagara* left to-day for home; we sent our mails and good wishes with her, and felt rather lonely when this noble frigate was gone.

March 5th. The *Rhode Island* arrived, after having been to Galveston, Texas, visiting our ships as she passed them. On her way home she is to call among the blockaders, carrying home the sick and leaving stores. We put four patients aboard her for home. In the evening the U. S. sloop-of-war *Richmond* arrived from home; also one or two gunboats. Thus the great fleet detailed to our flag-officer's command is slowly gathering in.

March 7th. Weighed anchor for the mouth of the Mississippi River; arrived in the evening, where we found the *Pensacola* and *Brooklyn* at Pass à l'Outre on the blockade. Our object in coming here was to go up the river, with the subsequent view of capturing New Orleans. Preparations were immediately made to cross the bar, a constantly shifting mud bank at the mouth of each pass of the Mississippi.

March 8th. This afternoon the *Brooklyn* made an attempt to cross the bar, being led by a gunboat, but the *Brooklyn* grounded, and after persevering with commendable zeal gave it up for the day. The men are grinding their cutlasses, and making other preparations of a warlike character.

March 9th. The *Brooklyn* tried all day, but with no effect, to cross the barrier before us. Capt. Bell went up the river in the gunboat *Winona* on a reconnoissance, and this evening came down with five prisoners, who were duly examined by the flag-officer, who after examination discharged them as neutrals.

March 11th. After failing to get up the river at this Pass we to-day steamed round to South-West Pass to try the depth of water there. We found the U. S. steam frigate *Colorado* here, besides several transports. On the following day the *Brooklyn* went over this bar and anchored on the other side. The *Hartford* followed on the 13th and all proceeded to Pilot Town, a little settlement just above the mouth of the Pass. Here it was decided to strip the ship for action; this occupied the 14th. We sent a guard of marines ashore to protect our property, and the flag which was raised on the lookout by Lieut. Kautz, Lieut. Broome of the marines, and Mr. Osbon; the guns were all shotted, and preparations made for any demonstration of the enemy.

March 15th. Went up to the head of the Passes, which is eighteen miles from the mouth. The rumor prevails that we here wait for Capt. Porter's mortar fleet. This is a dreary place, but somewhat pleasanter than below; where nothing was to be seen but mud, muddy water, and huge fog banks.

March 19th. Thirteen sail of Capt. Porter's fleet arrived today, being towed up the river by tugboats, and immediately taken to Pilot Town to dismantle. As business is monotonous at this season, our journal occasionally skips a few days.

March 29th. Nothing of importance is occurring now-a-days to mark one day from another. Yesterday, Capt. Bell, with the gunboats *Kennebeck*, *Wissahickon* and *Winona*, ascended the river to the forts, when Fort Jackson opened fire on them, and after firing about one hundred rounds at us our vessels hauled off. They discovered the position of the defenses, also a chain stretched across the river just below Forts Jackson and St. Philip, on eight schooners anchored between the forts. Our squadron is still gradually collecting. Capt. Porter's mortar fleet is already here, but our large ships are not all over the bar.

March 31st. Discovered a portion of a submarine telegraph cable across the river directly under our ship. The cable was destroyed, and a sample brought on board ship.

April 3d. The *Connecticut* arrived from home with mails and fresh provisions for the squadron, all of which were acceptable, and many a sailor's heart was gladdened by a letter from home.

April 8th. Was signalized by the mortar fleet, twenty-two in number, arriving from Pilot Town, where they had gone to be stripped of their rigging. They looked very pretty as they ranged along the shore in line of battle, with their flagship, the *Harriet Lane*, at their head. We look for a great noise from them before long.

April 15th. Yesterday a few vessels went up the river, and today the most of those remaining followed, including all of the mortar fleet. They "came to" just below range of the enemy's guns at the fort.

April 16th. The remainder of the vessels, including the *Hartford*, followed up the river, and anchored at the head of the fleet.

April 17th. Was spent in making preparations for the ensuing battle. The mortar boats were towed within range, and the tops of their masts dressed with green boughs from the adjacent woods, some having a whole broadside covered, but most of them with only their masts covered. In this condition they reminded one of a holiday scene rather than the stern preparations of battle.

April 18th. In order to understand the proceedings of our fleet fully, it will be necessary to explain the position of the enemy. Forts Jackson and St. Philip are situated on a short bend of the river, some forty miles from its mouth, Fort Jackson occupying the right bank and being the principal fort, and the other fort being situated opposite and a little below Jackson. A chain had been stretched across the river on eight schooners, and guarded by a water battery at its extremity. This, with the forts which mounted in the aggregate more than two hundred guns, was considered impregnable and impassable. This morning early the mortar boats were placed in position, and immediately opened fire on the forts, mostly engaging Fort Jackson. We were answered from the forts, but both parties fired slowly and endeavored to get the range, which was in distance some two to two and a half miles. In the meantime our advance fleet of gunboats moved up under cover of the point in the river's bend, and in turn dealt a few blows, all the time changing their position and dropping down with the current. In the evening a large fire in Fort Jackson gave evidence of the effect of our shells, and at night we hauled off our gunboats and ceased firing.

April 20th. The firing of yesterday was kept up all last night, and to appearances with considerable success. As the evening advanced the scene from the mortar boats rapidly increased in interest; as the shells left the gun the track of them through the air was distinctly visible, and the shots were quite accurate. This morning a deserter from Fort Jackson came aboard to visit the Commodore. He was a Pennsylvanian by birth, and had formerly been attached to Dan Rice's great shows. He stated that many of our shells lodged and bursted within the fort, much defacing it, and killing and wounding several men; also that the large fire reported in that vicinity was really in the fort, and during the excitement of putting out a second one he had escaped through an embrasure created by our firing.

Preparations were made for destroying the rebel chain by dismasting two of our gunboats, in order the more effectually to conceal them from view. At 10 o'clock, P. M., the *Itasca* got under way and steamed up to the chain in charge of Capt. Henry H. Bell. They were no sooner there than discovered, and fired upon with spirit, but owing to the darkness of the night no damage was done to them. During this period green, red, and blue lights went the rounds of our fleet, and the mortar boats opened with vigor, firing so fast that six to seven shells could be seen coursing through the air at once.

April 21st. At 1 o'clock this morning our gunboats returned, having succeeded in cutting the chain and setting two schooners adrift. At 3 o'clock all hands were aroused to ward off a large fire raft which among many others the enemy had sent adrift for our destruction, but like its predecessors it passed by harmless.

April 22d. A serious accident occurred this evening severely wounding five of our crew. A submerged vessel drifted upon our cable with such force as to tear it from its fastenings, breaking the pawls from the capstan. As this chain was connected with the capstan, and the bars shipped, they were whirled around with great velocity, knocking down several men. These men sustained severe contusions; one suffered the fracture of the forearm, and another was struck in the stomach, nearly killing him outright. Fire rafts appeared to-night, but did no damage.

April 24th. This morning was destined to be recorded in history as the day on which occurred the most brilliant naval feat ever accomplished. It had been decided to run past the forts without stopping, and accordingly, at two o'clock A. M., all hands were quietly turned out, hammocks lashed, and everything put in order, while two red lights from our peak gave the signal for the squadron to get under way.

The squadron was divided into three divisions under the commands of Flag Officer Farragut, Capt. Bailey, and Capt. Bell. The night was pleasant and starlight, and as we moved away the morning moon came looming up from behind the trees. Twenty minutes brought us within range of the enemy's guns, which were immediately opened upon us. Our men lay down on the decks till our guns could be brought to bear. The forts, mounting in the aggregate some two hundred and twenty guns, were soon in full blast upon us, and we returned the fire with decision and effect, making the action general and terrible. The forts, only three quarters of a mile apart, gave our ships shot and shell on both sides at once, while our ships sent back grape, canister, shrapnell, and shells, besides using our howitzers from our tops, where they had been mounted. On reaching the forts we were assailed by twenty of the enemy's gunboats and rams, but we made short work of them, sinking some, and burning nearly all of them.

A shell entered our starboard beam, cutting off our cable passing through eighteen inches of oak, and after tearing the armory down, exploded at the main hatch, killing one man instantly, and severely wounding three or four others; another entered the muzzle of a gun, breaking the lip, which killed the sponger, who was in the act of ramming home a cartridge. At this time we ran aground, when the ram *Manassas* forced a fire raft against our port quarter for the purpose of destroying us, but owing to the superhumane fforts of the officers and crew it was cast off and sent floating down the river. Our mizzen rigging was burnt, and the ship considerably charred, but we providentially escaped, and in a few minutes got afloat by backing down towards the enemy's forts, while they played away upon us beautifully.

After an hour and twenty minutes action we passed beyond reach of the rebel guns, and ceased firing. We came to our anchor at the quarantine grounds at about five o'clock, the river banks being lined on either side with burning steamers.

The ram *Manassas* had followed us up some distance, and now the old frigate *Mississippi* turned about to run her down, but the ram ran her nose into the mud, and the *Mississippi* in three broadsides crippled her, and she drifted down the river, while her crew escaped. One of our gunboats, the *Varuna*, after destroying five or six of the enemy's steamers was herself sunk, and was run aground with some loss of life. Our loss was some thirty in killed and one hundred wounded. The enemy's loss was five or six hundred, while their dead and wounded were burned in their steamers. Two of our gunboats were obliged to put back, one with a shot through her boilers, and the other disabled. Among the ships which passed the forts were the following: Flag ship *Hartford*, *Brooklyn*, *Pensacola*, *Richmond*, and the old frigate *Mississippi*, *Iroquois, and Oneida.* Gunboats *Varuna*, *Wissahickon*, *Cayuga*, *Katadin, and Pinola.* After taking prisoners from Camp Chalmette we started for New Orleans. White flags were waving in all directions, and as we proceeded the plantations and river banks presented a scene truly beautiful, being at a time of year when nature puts on her best attire. Some of the dwellings looked like castles, and bore evidence of age, being usually surrounded by large trees; each had attached its double row of negro dwellings, regularly laid out and interspersed with trees. We ran up near the English Turn, and anchored for the night unmolested.

April 25th. Left our anchorage early and proceeded up the river, keeping constantly on the alert for a battery which had been reported in this vicinity. We found the batteries some five or six miles below New Orleans called the Chalmette batteries, and consisting of some ten to fifteen guns. They opened upon us before we could get range of them, and we passed steadily on amid a shower of shell, and when within range gave them a broadside that sent them flying from their guns.

After an action of some thirty minutes all was quiet again, and, strange to say, none were injured except two, who fell overboard. As we passed on towards the city we were met by burning ships of all kinds; large ships were fired and cut adrift to float upon us, while others were burned at the levee. The destruction of property was immense, and hardly a ship or steamer escaped the flames. We anchored abreast of the city about 1 o'clock, P. M., amid a drenching rain, and the Flag Officer sent ashore a demand for the surrender of the city by Captain Bailey. The levee was thronged with people, and a party who waved a white flag and cheered for the Union thus created a terrible riot, and several persons were killed.

A rebel ram was burned and sunk at the levee, and the new floating battery *Mississippi*, of immense strength and proportions, was destroyed by fire and floated by us down the river.

April 26th. The Mayor of the city has surrendered it to Flag-officer Farragut, and a battalion of marines, under Capt. J. L. Broome, went ashore to raise the Stars and Stripes, but were opposed by the citizens and returned to the ship. In the afternoon we went up to Carrollton and captured sixty or eighty guns without firing a shot, they having been deserted and the gun carriages destroyed.

April 29th. We have been lying quietly at our anchorage here for two or three days, negotiating about the city and its flag and transfer. The river is alive with steamers which our people have taken possession of, and are gliding about seemingly practicing for duty by-and-by; among others, a fine steamer, the *Tennessee*, has been taken possession of and will doubtless prove quite a prize for us. The rebel gunboat *McRae* came up from the forts with a flag of truce, asking permission to bury her dead, but instead, watched her chance and scuttled her in deep water.

This morning a gunboat from the forts brought the pleasing intelligence that Forts Jackson and St. Philip had both surrendered to our forces below, and that a powerful floating battery, mounting eighteen guns and covered with railroad iron, had been fired and drifted down the river and blown up. This intelligence called all hands into the rigging, and they gave three times three cheers for the Union. At nine o'clock A. M., the marines of the squadron, under the command of Capt. J. L. Broome, went ashore to hoist the flag, backed by the howitzers; they proceeded to the Custom House and gave the Star-Spangled Banner to the breeze; thence they went to the Council House and lowered the State flag and brought it aboard as a trophy. Crowds of people frequent the levee to gaze on the shipping from day to day.

At 6:30 A. M., Capt. Bailey brought word up from below, that both forts had surrendered, and the Stars and Stripes were waving over them. At 3 P. M., Mr. Osbon, Flag Lieutenant, left the ship to go on board the gunboat *Cayuga*; as he was leaving, gave him three cheers. *Cayuga*, Capt. Bailey in command, went down the river, bound North with dispatches. Manned the rigging, and cheered ship.

April 30th. At 2 P. M., a steamer came up and landed the prisoners from the forts. This day, between the hours of ten and twelve o'clock, the carpenter of the fleet held a survey on this ship, and reported her not seaworthy, on account of a shot under her starboard counter.

May 1st. To-day General Butler's troops arrived to the number of some three thousand, in various craft: first came the *Mississippi*, a large screw steamer, literally so thronged with soldiers that they were hanging to the jibboom and almost every other conceivable part of the ship; after her the *Miami*; then a large ship and the river steamer *Diana*, all well filled with soldiers, and as they passed our ships cheer upon cheer rent the air, while a band discoursed music to us.

May 2d. In the midst of the excitement the U. S. steam transport *Rhode Island* came in with a large mail, which gladdened many a heart as they read letters from friends at home. This afternoon a collision took place between the *Brooklyn* and a gunboat, the latter drifting afoul of the former, when she dragged her anchor and both dropped down the stream; after going half a mile they were disengaged with the loss of the gunboat's smoke pipe, foremast and quarter boat.

May 3d. A serious accident occurred this evening, resulting in wounding more than twenty men. The men were heaving up anchor when the ship swung off with the current, bringing up on the cable with such violence as to whirl the men from the bars, breaking the pawls of the capstan, and the bars throwing the men in all directions. The injuries were one dislocated shoulder, one fractured fore-arm, one do. finger, one do. skull, one do. jaw, and many jammed, bruised and bleeding.

May 7th. We weighed anchor this afternoon for up the river, and stopped for the night at a plantation some ten miles above Carrollton and twenty above the city. The scenery along here is perfectly beautiful, reminding one of pleasant scenes at home.

May 8th. Weighed anchor early and proceeded up the river. The same succession of beauties met the eye at every turn. In the afternoon met a gunboat from Vicksburg with news from our vessels at that place.

May 9th. Arrived at Baton Rouge in the afternoon, where we found the *Brooklyn and Iroquois.* This city is the capital of Louisiana, and a very pleasant place, with some four or five thousand inhabitants. The capitol is a beautiful building; also an asylum for the insane. There are also here the state prison and U. S. Arsenal. The city is elevated some twenty feet above the river, and the buildings roofed with slate.

May 13th. We have been lying here several days coaling ship, &c., while our officers have been going ashore both on business and pleasure. This afternoon two steamers arrived from New Orleans loaded with troops for this place; they landed, and after parading the streets for a couple of hours returned to their boats for the night.

May 14th. We weighed anchor early for Vicksburg; at noon we came upon an island which divided the river into two channels. We took the right and pushed along within three rods of the trees, and could hear the birds singing in them. Nothing of note occurred until two o'clock P. M., when in making a short turn we ran aground, but by properly disposing of the crew we were soon afloat and passing along as gaily as ever; we ran on till eight P. M., when in trying to lay the ship to out of the current she was run high aground; the night was occupied in trying to get her afloat, but without success.

May 15th. Was spent in exertions to get our ship afloat. A gunboat was dispatched for a lighter, and we commenced discharging our battery on board a gunboat, and shell on board a steamer, also coal into a lighter.

May 16th. After discharging through the night a line was attached to a kedge off our quarter, and a gunboat hauling at the same time, started her from the sand, and at ten o'clock the *Hartford* was again a thing of life. The day was spent in reloading.

May 17th. Got under way at five o'clock, A. M., and steamed along very slowly, owing to our burning bituminous coal, of which we had taken a little. At about noon we were obliged to anchor to get up steam, and as usual a boat put off to the nearest house for officers' stores. Happening to anchor in an eddy, we were in imminent danger of being dashed on the levee. At another time, when we anchored in seventy fathoms of water, the ship continued to whirl round and round until we again weighed. We were soon under way again, and having substituted anthracite coal for the other, had no further difficulty. The banks were lined with cotton, and the river was so high that the levee was seldom visible; private dwellings were partly submerged, and in many instances all that could be seen of buildings was their roofs peering out of the water, and reminding one of the late style of rams; in fact, the river was said to be higher than before known for thirty years.

We frequently came upon portions of the river which seemed to terminate the great stream, and surrounded it on all sides with earth and trees; at such a place we arrived near sunset, and anchored for the night, though not until we had discovered that the stream continued. A boat went ashore for fresh meat, and returned about one o'clock, A. M., with a slaughtered bull and some mutton, for which, as usual, we paid gold.

May 18th. Found us under way early, expecting to reach Natchez in the course of the day. About noon the order was given to get the anchor ready for letting go, and we looked ahead for an anchorage. In one of the everlasting bends of the river, on a bluff forty or fifty feet high, could be seen a few houses, and others on the river banks below, with a road running from one group to the other upon almost perpendicular banks. This was Natchez, and here we anchored alongside the sloops-of-war *Brooklyn* and *Richmond*, which had been here several days waiting for us. Natchez is not discernible from the river, as it lies mainly over the hill, back from the river; but, from present appearances, we should judge it to be a rather lazy city.

May 19th. We left Natchez this morning and went up some fifteen miles, followed by the other ships, and stopped in the woods. In the afternoon the steamer *Laurel Hill* arrived and passed from below with troops, and the gunboat *Kennebec* came down from Vicksburg with news. At eight P. M., William Preston, signal-quartermaster, died of apoplexy induced by the heat, after an illness of three days.

May 20th. The quartermaster was buried ashore this morning, after which we got under way and proceeded up some thirty miles, where we found the river again divided by an island, and the *Brooklyn, Richmond* and *Iroquois* having preceded us and taken the wrong channel, the two former ones had run aground. We lay by till morning, in the meantime sounding; the *Brooklyn* soon got off.

May 21st. We got under way early, leaving the *Iroquois* aground, and ran up to Grand Gulf, where we are to wait for orders from the Flag Officer who has gone to Vicksburg. We saw much cotton afloat to-day, and the country nearly all overflowed by the turbid waters of the Mississippi.

May 24th. We left Grand Gulf on the 23d, at which time the Flag Officer joined us, and arrived four miles below Vicksburg at four o'clock, P. M., where we found several gunboats awaiting our arrival. We swelled the number here to eleven vessels of war. The city is situated on a bluff perhaps sixty feet high, and they have a battery on the hill, and another one below, but we do not know the number of guns mounted; they also have a ram to protect them, besides large numbers of troops behind the city. The *Kennebec,* with the several captains of the fleet, went up to reconnoitre, and on returning was saluted by the ram with a shot which fell far short.

May 26th. Another reconnoissance took place yesterday, but although the gunboats went very near the rebel batteries no firing took place. This morning all hands were surprised with the intelligence that no attack was to be made on the city at present, and that our large ships would again drop down the river. This is said to be caused by the fact that the position of the rebel guns renders the attack dangerous to our large ships, and that we could not at present occupy the place, if taken. The *Richmond* started early down the river, followed by the *Brooklyn* and at ten o'clock we got under way with the gunboat *Kennebec,* leaving eight vessels behind in charge of Capt. Palmer of the *Iroquois.* We also had in company, or rather ahead of us, two steamers loaded with troops. Nothing transpired to check our rapid passage until the steamers, in passing Grand Gulf, were fired upon by rebel light artillery; we accordingly wheeled round, and in company with the *Brooklyn* went back for satisfaction. The troops were landed, and they drove the enemy out of the town with slight loss, while we proceeded down and passed the night a few miles above Natchez, where were four of our coal transports.

May 27th. Got under way, and taking a coal schooner alongside, proceeded on our way. Passed Natchez at eleven thirty, A. M., without stoppage, and ran all day without any occurrence of note, anchoring by a plantation, and sending ashore for fresh provisions at sunset.

May 28th. During the night the levee broke opposite to our ship, and the water is running through at a fearful rate, threatening to flood the surrounding plantations. We weighed early, and arrived at Baton Rouge at ten o'clock, A. M. Everything looked quiet, and the dingey was sent ashore with Chief Engineer Kimball, manned by four boys. On landing at the levee, they were attacked by a body of guerilla cavalry, and immediately shoved off; but the guerillas poured a volley of slugs and shot into the boat, wounding the Chief Engineer and two of the boys. They then scampered off on horseback as fast as they could go, while our boat was picked up by a gunboat which was anchored below us. We immediately opened our battery on them, raking the streets and firing some twenty shots, when the men were with difficulty compelled to cease firing. The excitement on board our ship was intense, and each man desired to see the city in ashes. During the afternoon, several Northern ladies came off for protection, and the Mayor of the city, with those of secesh proclivities, had already skedaddled, leaving the place nearly desolate.

May 29th. Early this morning the *Brooklyn*, with her attendants, arrived from up the river, when the Flag Officer ordered the troops, fifteen hundred in number, ashore to watch the city, while we broke out of our ship's hold nearly all of our provisions for their use. At ten o'clock the *Brooklyn* got under way for New Orleans, and we soon followed, leaving two gunboats to guard the place by water. We anchored at night as usual, and on the morning had the misfortune to lose our anchor by the parting of the chain. We got under way early, and reached New Orleans a little after noon, where we found a display of shipping not unlike the happiest days of the Crescent City.

There were some half dozen men-of-war here, also the U. S. mail packet *Ocean Queen*, a large and splendid ship; also the U. S. transport *Connecticut*, with a mail for us, and a large number of transports and merchantmen lining the levee, while the merchant steamers flying about the river created a lively and pleasing appearance. On this passage, Quartermaster Donnelly died of apoplexy, induced by the heat of the sun and season, being the second case from the same cause. We lay here for more than a week, during which time steamships were constantly arriving from the North, bringing mails, dispatches, &c., and a corresponding number departed, among them the U. S. sloop-of-war *Dacotah*.

On the 8th of June, the Flag Officer having received the proper authority, once more turned the *Hartford* towards Vicksburg, followed by the *Richmond*—the *Brooklyn* being detained, but soon followed. We anchored near sunset, alongside the U. S. steam transport *Tennessee*, which had got aground. During the night the *Brooklyn* arrived, in company with several river steamers with troops. On the following morning two steamers fastened to the *Tennessee*, to tow her off, while we passed on, and arrived without accident at Baton Rouge on the 10th, where we found everything going off quietly. We lay here nearly ten days, during which time the mortar schooners of Capt. Porter's fleet had passed by us, and having left one, we on the 19th took it in tow and started for Vicksburg. We proceeded with moderate speed and success until the 21st, in the evening, when we unexpectedly ran hard aground. Our attendant steamers immediately came up to our assistance, and after laboring the entire night, succeeded in getting afloat the following morning at eleven o'clock. Continuing on we passed some high bluffs, on which we looked for rebel batteries and accordingly kept prepared for them, but we were not molested. We observe that the river is rapidly falling, having thus far receded some six feet.

We arrived at Vicksburg on the 25th, where we found the *Brooklyn* and *Richmond*, the gunboats, and mortar fleet; and, soon after arriving, an officer came on board from Commodore Davis's fleet, and communicated with Commodore Farragut. Davis, in our absence, had moved down the river, and now occupied a position just above Vicksburg.

Preparations were immediately made for an attack, by putting the mortars in position but they did not open until the evening of the 26th. On the following day they bombarded slowly the whole day. In the evening a council of Commanders determined to attack the place on the following morning. During the night the mortars were moved up to easy range, and on the 28th, before daylight, the mortars opened in earnest. The whole fleet now moved up to the attack.

Our ships were before the city, while the shells from the mortars were being hurled right over our heads, and, as battery after battery was unmasked from every conceivable position, the ridge of the bluff was one sheet of fire. The big ships sent in their broadsides, the mortars scores of shell, and all combined to make up a grand display and terrible conflict. After nearly two hours of hard fighting, our ships had nearly all passed the city, out of range, and the firing ceased.

On looking around I found the *Hartford* riddled from stem to stern; first a hole through her bow, then two through the side, one below water, then another through the bulwarks, another through the stern and cabin, and another through the smoke-pipe, &c., &c., the main topsail-yard cut in twain, and the rigging terribly cut fore and aft.

Our casualties in killed and wounded were light—one killed, and a dozen slightly wounded, including the Flag Officer and Capt. Broome of the marines—while the casualties of the fleet were less than a dozen in killed. The afternoon was devoted to burying the dead and communicating with the ram fleet belonging to Commodore Davis's division. From our anchorage we could see across the point of land to General Williams's camp and the transports below, and we immediately established communication with them. Here we spent the Fourth of July, which was celebrated by the booming of cannon from both fleets, and a volley of shells to the rebels. I visited the iron-clad gunboat *Benton*, which to me was quite a curiosity.

July 15th. Has changed the affairs of the fleet materially. Before daylight a firing of cannon had been heard up the river, and a gunboat had been dispatched to reconnoitre. As time passed, the firing neared us, and soon cannon balls could be seen dropping into the river below a bend which hid objects from our view. The enemy proved to be the rebel ram *Arkansas*, which had chased our gunboat down the Yazoo river, and now came booming along, firing at our ships as she came. As no danger was apprehended, our ships were all lying without steam, and so near together that for one to fire endangered the rest.

All hands were called to quarters, and the ram came on and passed us, while each vessel which could fire upon her, did so, but we were not able to sink or disable her. Preparations were immediately made to follow her, and on the same evening our ships got under way, resolved to run down by the batteries and destroy the ram if possible. We commenced firing about dark, the ball being opened by Commodore Davis's iron-clads, and in twenty minutes from the time of opening fire, we were in full blast. We passed slowly by the city, receiving fewer shots than formerly and being unable to discover the ram, which had been secreted behind a huge wharf-boat, and consequently we were unable in the darkness to harm her. We came to anchor below the city, and found our casualties to be, in killed three, and Captain Broome and Mr. Hoffman severely, and four of the crew slightly, wounded.

We lay here two or three days taking in coal, &c., and it was finally arranged that the iron-clad *Essex* should run down by the batteries, with a prospect of destroying the ram, and of relieving the wooden ships which had already been ordered down the river. Accordingly, on the morning of the 22d we got under way, and awaited the appearance from above, ready to attack the ram or assist the *Essex*, as the case might require. At six o'clock firing commenced, and soon the *Essex* appeared, followed by a small wooden ram, and proceeded down through the batteries, giving the ram a broadside as she passed her, while the whole rebel line opened upon her. I here witnessed a most sublime picture in naval operations,—a lone vessel running the gauntlet of some thirty cannon placed in the hillside, raining a shower of shot and shell thickly around her. She escaped, however, with the loss of one man killed, and a single shot through her armor.

We had now reached the 24th of July, and the climate had become deleterious to the health of our sailors, mostly in the shape of a malarious fever, which was prostrating a dozen a day. We had a sick list of about one hundred men, and we now most gladly started down the river, leaving the command with Commodore Davis. The mortar boats had previously been removed, and we now sailed for New Orleans.

We had a pleasant passage to New Orleans, where we arrived July 28th, and found the U. S. transport *Connecticut* awaiting us with a large mail. On this evening we had a heavy shower of rain, accompanied by heavy thunder and sharp lightning, purifying the air to a very pleasant degree. We now proceeded to coal ship preparatory to proceeding on our way. The sailors were here given liberty on shore—about eighty at a time—for twenty-four hours each. I here took a few hours to myself, and set foot on shore for the first time in six months. I had a very limited view of a portion of the city, and came back to the ship after a stay of four hours.

On the night of the 25th intelligence arrived from Baton Rouge that the rebels had made an attack on the latter place and, killing General Williams, had been repulsed. The *Hartford* was immediately turned up the river for Baton Rouge. On our passage we lost our orderly sergeant of marines, who died of bilious colic; we buried him at the latter place. On arriving we learned that a hard battle had been fought, and that the rebel ram *Arkansas* had been attacked and destroyed. As the rebels had left the place, and the *Arkansas* had ceased to trouble us, we turned our ship, and for the last time sailed down the stream. Things went quietly until arriving at Donaldsonville, where we came to, and after bombarding the little village for an hour, sent a few boats ashore and burned the place to the ground. This act was occasioned by guerrilla bands repeatedly firing upon our transports, and after being warned, the Commodore determined to make an example of it. Nothing in the line of eatables was found here, but large quantities of choice wines were discovered, of which our sailors partook freely, notwithstanding their fear of poison.

We arrived at New Orleans on the following day, where we remained several days.

On the 10th August, Commander Wainwright died, after an illness of two weeks. His remains were placed in a metallic coffin and sent on board the U. S. steamer *Miami*, which steamer carried them to Washington, D. C.

We sailed August 13th from New Orleans, and reached Forts Jackson and St. Philip, where we remained over night, and received a salute for the Admiral. We got under way on the following morning, and proceeded to Pilot Town. We found several fine U. S. ships here, among them the U. S. ship *Pampero*, with which we slightly collided, doing little damage. We here took in our spare spars and rigging, which we had stripped off on entering the river, and also removed the chain cable from our ship's side.

On the 16th we left for Ship Island, getting aground on the bar as we went out, and arrived off Ship Island on the same evening. We went into port on the following morning, and found lying here the U. S. frigate *Potomac*, and U. S. sloop-of-war *Richmond*. The *Rhode Island* arrived on the 19th, and we left the same day for Pensacola, via Mobile Bay. On arriving off Mobile we found on the blockade the U. S. frigate *Susquehanna*, with several gunboats. We received and returned a salute from the *Susquehanna*, and passed on to Pensacola. We arrived off the place in the evening, and went into the harbor on the following morning, and moored the ship off the Navy Yard.

August 27th. At six P. M., called all hands to muster, when Lieutenant Commander James S. Thornton transferred the command of this ship to Captain James S. Palmer, late of the *Iroquois*, which was the occasion of a few remarks from Capt. Palmer to the ship's company. At nine P. M. Lieutenant Com. Thornton left the ship, to take command of the gunboat *Winona*.

November 7th. It is just two months and eighteen days since we first cast our anchor in Pensacola Bay. Up to the present time nothing has occurred worthy of note. It was the general impression on our arrival here that we came to Pensacola for the purpose of making every necessary preparation for an attack upon Mobile. All of the vessels attached to our fleet required more or less repairing, particularly the old *Hartford*, but now it seems the programme for the season is changed, and we are once more to pay our compliments to the old Mississippi river. Our Admiral has been informed by the commanding officer whom we left in the river to guard the city, that the rebels are building more batteries along the banks of the river some miles above the city. We are informed that they are strongly fortifying Port Hudson, which is one hundred and sixty-four miles above New Orleans, situated on high bluffs similar to Vicksburg. I sincerely hope that if we are called upon to do more fighting in this vicinity, as I presume we shall according to the aspect of things at present, then may we clean them out thoroughly.

Our ship is once more under way, bound for New Orleans. This morning at ten o'clock we weighed anchor, and started ahead, followed by the U. S. steam sloop *Richmond*, and U. S. transport *Tennessee*. Arrived off Mobile at six P. M., found the U. S. sloop of war *Brooklyn* at anchor here, which vessel has been lying here for some time, doing blockade duty. We came to here, while Capt. Bell of the *Brooklyn* came on board to report to the Admiral. At eight P. M., started ahead, shaped our course for South-West Pass, Mississippi.

November 8th. Came to anchor off South-West Pass at nine A. M. We were saluted with thirteen guns by a large French man-of-war which was lying to anchor at this place. We returned the salute. At three thirty P. M., *Richmond* got under way and attempted to cross the bar, but unfortunately she grounded; signalized for steamer *Tennessee* to assist in getting her over; after about two hours hard working they succeeded in passing over; in the meantime we got under way and steamed over the bar without any difficulty.

Again in the old Mississippi river. At six forty-five P. M., passed the steamer *Potomac* going down, bound for New York. At ten P. M., arrived at the forts; here a gun was fired as a signal for us to come to; after ascertaining who we were we were allowed to pass on. It will be remembered that on the eventful morning of April 24th, 1862, there was more than one gun fired at us as a signal for us to come to. Not deeming it expedient to stop, we continued on our course. Our conduct in this particular was considered by those occupying Forts Jackson and St. Philip at that time impudent and insulting in the extreme. Finding that we took no heed to the gun which they first fired, they immediately fired another, and another. Thinking therefore, that we had been very finely saluted, it was considered proper that we should return it, so accordingly, finding that our battery was in order and in fine trim, we paid our compliments to Mr. Secesh by giving them a few broadsides, making brick and mortar fly in all directions. Not liking our style altogether, the firing soon became general, and it was not long before it was ascertained that somebody was missing. However, continuing on our course we passed the quarantine grounds at eleven P. M. Having a very good pilot on board, we were able to run all night, reaching the city on the following morning.

November 9th. Arrived off the city of New Orleans at noon, and came to anchor. Here we were saluted again by a French and an English man-of-war which were laying at anchor here. We are once more occupying our old position as the Flag Ship. As a matter of course all business for the fleet is transacted on board of this ship. As soon as we dropped our anchor the business began. All commanding officers attached to vessels lying here come on board to report to the Admiral. The city looks about as it did when we left, with one exception; there seems to be a little more business going on about the levees; there are also more vessels in port than when we left here.

November 10th. Everything quiet; weather clear and pleasant. This morning a mail steamer arrived from the North.

November 11th. The Admiral left the ship to go on board the English sloop-of-war *Rinaldo*. At noon the Englishman manned yards for Rear Admiral Farragut.

November 13th. To-day the French Admiral came on board. Saluted him as he was leaving, with thirteen guns, which the French steamer returned.

November 19th. Since my last entry nothing has occurred worthy of note. This morning, at nine o'clock, we hoisted the Spanish flag at our fore, in honor of the Queen of Spain's birthday.

December 14th. Astounding intelligence reached us through a telegram to the Admiral, stating that Major General Banks, with his entire expedition, was on the river coming up to the city. The *North Star* came up to the lower part of the city and landed the General. General Banks comes to supersede Major General Butler in command of the Gulf Department, and will perhaps at this stage of affairs serve the interests of the Government better than Butler, who is much the harsher man, could. When General Butler first took charge of affairs here a strict, energetic man was needed,— one who would not hesitate an instant to punish severely the first act of insubordination. Butler was the man; but latterly this severity is uncalled for, and the public need a milder rule, and General Banks in my opinion is the better man for such.

December 15th. To-day several fine steamers belonging to Banks' expedition arrived, loaded with troops; all transports, as they arrive, lay off in the stream.

December 16th. To-day six more steamers arrived loaded with troops, and as they passed our ship cheer upon cheer rent the air, while a brass band discoursed splendid music.

December 17th. This afternoon, at two o'clock, Major-General Banks and Brigadier-General Augur, with their staffs, visited the ship. Our Admiral and Commodore seemed highly pleased to meet with them; they remained on board about two hours. As they were leaving, a salute of thirteen guns was fired.

December 24th. To-day Major-General Butler and Brigadier-General Shepley visited the ship. At eleven A. M., General Butler left the ship in the barge, and went on board the steamer *S. R. Spaulding*, which is to convey him North. Saluted him with thirteen guns; also cheered ship. The *Spaulding* went down the river as soon as General Butler arrived on board. At three P. M., French Admiral visited the ship.

One year has nearly elapsed since we weighed anchor at Philadelphia, and in that space of time Admiral Farragut has accomplished what perhaps no other man in the U. S. Navy could have done, viz., opened the way to New Orleans. True, Vicksburg is yet in the way of the free navigation of the Mississippi river, yet that fact detracts not one iota from the credit due to the brave old man. The original object of the expedition was simply the reduction of Forts Jackson and St. Philip, and the fortifications supposed to be placed on the river up to the city of New Orleans; but after the splendid success that crowned the efforts of the fleet, the Government issued the order that Vicksburg should be attacked, which was accordingly done, the fleet passing and repassing it; and it was patent to every intelligent eye, that had there been troops sent to garrison the place, the batteries opposed to us could easily have been carried under the fire that would have been brought to bear from the shipping. Porter's iron fleet then formed a junction with us, and as this was their proper district we withdrew, having cleared the Mississippi river for the distance of *four hundred miles, and thereby thrown open to commerce an immense district of the richest portion of the South.*

Of the smaller places that were conquered under the direction of Admiral Farragut no mention need here be made, *the crowning deed was done in the first battle,* and besides, are not "all these mentioned in the Chronicles."

In the selection of the officers in charge of the different departments of the expedition, Government has been very fortunate. They all thoroughly understood their work, and heartily co-operated in their efforts to overcome the enemy. The crews of the vessels are men that do honor to their commanders,—hardy, brave and willing, they need no urging, and are entitled to the motto, *Semper paratus.*

The expedition has been so fortunate as not to encounter that infectious disease, yellow fever,—more to be feared by unacclimated persons than the fiercest battles. The excellent sanitary regulations of the fleet, by Dr. Foltz, has caused the mortality from disease to be less than the most sanguine could have hoped. The loss of life in battle has been very small, all things being taken into consideration, although the expedition has been the most fortunate of the war, owing, under Providence, to Rear-Admiral Farragut, and his meritorious and intelligent officers.

New Orleans, January 1st, 1863. Nothing of importance has occurred this day.

January 3d. To-day, at one o'clock, we were honored with a visit from Major-General Banks and Brigadier-General Weitzel.

Sunday morning, January 4th. This morning, at ten thirty, prayers were read on the quarter-deck, after which a general muster of the crew took place. To-day we received a mail from home by the U. S. steamer *Circassian.*

January 12th. Nothing of importance is occurring now-a-days to mark one day from another.

January 16th. This morning, at ten o'clock, the officers, twelve men, and marine guard of this ship went on shore to attend the funeral of Lieutenant-Commander T. McKean Buchanan, who was killed in action by the rebels in Berwick's Bay, while commanding the *Calhoun* on Jan. 14th, 1863. To-day we received another mail from home, which gladdened the hearts of many.

Feb. 6th. Since my last entry nothing has occurred worthy of note. This morning at ten thirty all hands were called to up anchor; got under way and stood down the river; at seven P. M., came to anchor off Pilot Town.

Pilot Town, Feb. 9th. We have been lying to anchor here for over two days, for the reason that there has not been sufficient depth of water on the bar to admit of our crossing. At eleven thirty A. M., pilot came on board and reported water enough. At noon, got under way and steamed down. Unfortunately for us, in attempting to cross the bar at South-West Pass we ran the ship hard aground.

Feb. 10th. Still aground; at two P. M., succeeded in getting off by the assistance of two river tugboats which had been sent to our assistance; in the meantime the steamer *Che Kiang* had been sent down the river with despatches for the Admiral to return to the city. Just as we got nicely over the bar, the despatches were brought on board; the ship was immediately turned around, and back we started again, and in attempting to cross the bar the second time we grounded; the tugboats fastened to us again the *Che Kiang* hitched on, and with considerable difficulty we succeeded in getting over. If we had not been so unfortunate as to run our ship's nose into the mud in our first attempt at crossing the bar, the *Che Kiang*, in my opinion, would have had a fine time in overhauling us, and at the same time we might have enjoyed a fine sea breeze.

Feb. 11th, nine thirty A. M. Arrived off the city and brought the ship to anchor.

Feb. 17th. To-day the U. S. steamer *Mississippi* got under way with a schooner in tow and proceeded up the river.

Feb. 22d. We fired a salute to-day, of seventeen guns, in honor of the birth-day of Washington.

March 1st. This morning, at ten thirty, had public worship on the quarter-deck, after which a general muster of the crew took place. Weather clear and pleasant.

March 2nd. To-day we have been engaged in coaling ship.

March 9th. At ten A. M. called all hands to up anchor. At ten forty-five A. M., got under way, steaming up the river, followed by the U. S. steam sloop-of-war *Richmond* and *Monongahela*; while steaming up the river, the men were employed in snaking down the rigging. At seven P. M. brought the ship to anchor for the night.

March 10th. At five thirty A. M. got under way; started ahead, steaming up the river. At nine A. M. beat to quarters, passed Donaldsonville; at this place a few companies of General Banks's army were encamped. As our ship passed on, we were saluted by the soldiers on shore. At six P. M. brought ship to anchor off Manchac.

March 11th. At five-thirty A. M. got under way, and continued on up the river. At nine A. M. brought ship to anchor off the city of Baton Rouge, La. The crew have been employed to-day coaling ship.

March 12th. The *Genesee* went up the river to-day with two mortar schooners in tow.

March 13th. To-day the gunboat *Sachem* started up the river, also two transports loaded with troops. The day has been spent in getting the ship ready for action. This afternoon, army signal officers came on board to accompany us up the river. Mortar vessels are moving up to take their positions for bombarding; at four P. M. we got under way, and started up the river, followed by the *Richmond*, *Mississippi*, *Monongahela*, and gunboat *Kineo*. As soon as the ships were got under way we beat to quarters.

The Admiral, Fleet Captain and Captain Palmer commanding, also Mr. Kimberly, executive officer, inspected the ship fore and aft, to see that all things were in readiness; at seven thirty P. M. came to anchor for the night, it being so very dark it was deemed necessary, as every precaution is required under the circumstances.

March 14th. This morning at five thirty, called all hands to up anchor, signalized the fleet to get under way, started ahead, ran some distance further up the river, came in sight of the batteries at Port Hudson; at seven thirty A. M., brought ship to anchor; the whole fleet came to anchor at the same time. Here we are able to command a view of the enemy's batteries; we are lying within four miles of them, just out of range of their guns. The mortar schooners are lying about one mile ahead of our ships, under cover of a point of land; in this position they will bombard the enemy; it is quite probable that an attack will be made to-night. This afternoon an officer came on board with dispatches from Gen. Banks. The mortars have opened fire upon the batteries, simply to get range. Another rebel steamer came down the river this afternoon, making five in all; they lay under cover of the batteries.

It is now decided to make an attack to-night. We took the small gunboat *Albatross* in tow; she was made fast to our port quarter. The *Richmond* and *Monongahela* had, each of them, a gunboat made fast to them also. This was done after dark, so that the enemy could not see our movements; at nine P. M., everything being in readiness, signals were made for the whole fleet to get under way, and follow us up; we beat to quarters, and waited for the fleet to form in line of battle. A very few minutes elapsed before we were all in motion, each vessel taking its respective station; at ten P. M., the tugboat *Reliance* came up with despatches for the Admiral; spoke, and sent her back to hasten the rear ships; at ten thirty *Richmond* reported rear ships moving up to station; we moved along very slowly and very cautiously; the night being so very dark, we endeavored to approach the enemy as near as possible without being seen. As soon as we were discovered, the enemy opened their batteries upon us. It was some time before we could get any of our guns to bear; as a matter of course, we were obliged to stand and take it; however, we kept on our course with but one object in view, "conquer or die." After being under fire of the enemy's guns for some time, we succeeded in getting our guns to bear, then the firing became general and fearful in the extreme; our ships were all in full blast. In the meantime, the mortar vessels, six in number, let drive their missiles of death. By this time, our ships had got right under the batteries, and in the thickest of the firing. Unfortunately we ran aground; it was not long, however, before we were afloat again, as full steam was applied, and we succeeded in backing off; the enemy, in the meantime, did their utmost to destroy our noble ship.

We were under fire of the enemy's guns one hour and ten minutes; our ship sustained more damage in this battle than any other we have been in yet. After we had passed by the batteries, our first duty was to ascertain the fate of our fleet; as it was so intensely dark, it was impossible to see the length of the ship from us; not many minutes elapsed before we were informed that the *Hartford*, and the gunboat which we had in tow, were the only vessels out of the whole fleet that had succeeded in passing by the batteries. We passed on out of range of their guns, and brought ship to anchor. What had become of the balance of our fleet, was now a mystery to us. It was very evident that our ships had met with a serious fate, or else some of them would have passed by. We could see from our anchorage a large fire raging below the batteries, supposed to be the side-wheel steamer *Mississippi*, from which a frequent number of explosions were heard.

Sunday morning, March 16th, two o'clock. The fighting is still going on with our ships below, and the mortars are still contesting with the enemy. In our action we lost one man killed, and two slightly wounded. Three o'clock A. M., one hour later; the firing below has ceased, enemy still in possession of their batteries. All hands were called to "splice the main brace." It will be remembered that we had some five or six of the enemy's steamers to contend with after passing their batteries, but we soon made them skedaddle, unable to close in with them on account of their superior speed. Nine A. M.—We nailed a placard on the remains of our launch, dated five miles above Port Hudson, stating our safe arrival, and sent it drifting down the river, with the expectation of our friends below intercepting it, as our communications with them were all cut off.

At ten thirty A. M. got under way again, in company of *Albatross*, and proceeded on up the river in search of the enemy. The day was very stormy and foggy, still we kept on our course, our pilot being one of the very best that ever traveled this river. Four P. M., brought ship to anchor for the night; the storm is still raging severely. Nine o'clock P. M. A light is reported from the masthead, coming down the river; the rattle is sprung, calling all hands to quarters; soon ascertained, however, that it was a light on shore. The night was one of the very worst that I ever experienced—dark, stormy, and we were expecting every moment to be attacked by the enemy's boats; the night passed over with great anxiety on the part of all hands.

March 16th. This morning at five thirty got under way, and steamed up the river in charge of the pilot. At seven A. M. two men came on board, and reported themselves as belonging to the original crew of the *Queen of the West*, having escaped from her after her capture by the rebels, since which time they have been concealed in the woods. At nine A. M. weighed and started on up, weather having cleared up so as to be able to see our way. At eleven thirty A. M. brought ship to anchor off the mouth of Red River. It is quite evident that there are a number of the enemy's gunboats up this river. This afternoon the ship's company have been engaged at target practice.

March 17th. This morning at four o'clock we left our anchorage at the mouth of Red River, and proceeded up the Mississippi. We arrived off Natchez at six P. M. and brought ship to anchor. This is our fifth appearance at this place. As soon as we arrived our Admiral sent a boat on shore under a flag of truce, with a despatch to the Mayor, stating that if our ship was fired into during the night, that he would burn the city down. The citizens at this place are of the strongest kind of secesh. We have been able through their daily journals, to see the regard which they have for us; and we are well aware that if there were no restraint placed upon the people at this place, they would instantly resort to some means to destroy our vessels as they pass up and down, or at least would make some effort towards it.

March 18th. This morning, at five o'clock, got under way, and proceeded on up the river, No act of violence occurred to our ship during last night while laying off Natchez. During the day the ship's company have been engaged in making preparations to prevent the enemy's steamers from coming alongside to board us, by securing chain cable out to the lower yard-arms; also preparing boarding nettings. At six P. M. came to anchor for the night, about seven miles below Grand Gulf.

March 19th. This morning we were taken a little by surprise. Not expecting to meet with any opposition along here, we were not altogether prepared for it, as we have been on all former occasions. As no fighting had been anticipated the watch below was allowed to sleep in their hammocks, while the watch on deck got the ship under way. At five A. M. weighed and started ahead, steaming along slowly, and at six forty-five, as we came within range of the enemy's guns, which they had mounted on high cliffs at this place, known as Grand Gulf, the enemy opened fire upon our ship, causing great excitement as a matter of course. We beat to quarters immediately; as soon as our guns could be brought to bear, we fired our broadside into the enemy's batteries, and not until we had fired our broadside guns did the watch below know of what was going on. The excitement of those below sleeping, being awakened from their sound slumbers by the report of guns right over their heads, and the enemy's shots striking the ship in many places, may be more easily imagined than described. We steamed ahead as rapidly as possible, and before our guns could be reloaded we had passed beyond range, although not altogether out of range of the enemy's guns. We endeavored to train our guns so as to pay them back in their own coin for the damage they had done us, but we were not able to do them any, as our ship had by this time passed too far beyond. The enemy continued to shell us at long range, and the only retaliation we could make was with one heavy rifled gun which we had mounted on the poop deck. The battle was of short duration, lasting altogether about thirty minutes. Our casualties were two killed, and five slightly wounded, while our ship sustained much damage. If we had been aware of the fact that the enemy had fortified this place, we would have been prepared for them, and it is quite probable that we would have done them much more damage than what we did. The enemy got the best of us this time; but as our sailors say it was not a square fight, and when we go down the river again we will show them what are the fighting qualities of the old *Hartford*. It is quite evident that they know something of them already, as Forts Jackson and St. Philip, the Chalmette batteries and Vicksburg, and lastly, Port Hudson can testify to this fact. However, we continued on our course up the river. We met with no further opposition, and at three forty-five P. M., brought ship to anchor twelve miles below Vicksburg, or three miles below Warrenton.

As soon as we came to anchor a small boat was seen approaching from ashore; soon ascertained that the boat contained four men, one of them a Lieutenant, the other a private belonging to our army; they were on picket duty. Seeing our ship approach they knew who we were, so accordingly they came on board to inform our Admiral of what they knew. We were very happy indeed to meet with friends. The Admiral immediately dispatched his secretary, Mr. Gabaudan, to communicate with Admiral Porter's fleet above Vicksburg. It is reported that we have an army of two hundred thousand men in the vicinity of Vicksburg. It is very probable that an attack will be made upon this place very soon. It is doubtful, however, whether we participate in the attack, as we are alone.

At five thirty P. M., called all hands to bury the dead; read the funeral services over the bodies of Charles Sweeney, seaman, and Dennis Driscoll, landsman; sent an officer on shore in charge of bodies to see them interred. The Lieutenant who came off to the ship in the small boat brought with him two prisoners; placed them in confinement on suspicion of being in rebel employ.

March 20th. Nothing has occurred to-day worthy of note. Rebel pickets have been seen all day on the opposite shore. Last night the mortar vessels above Vicksburg opened fire and shelled the city for about three hours.

March 21st. At nine A. M., got under way, went to quarters, and steamed up the river a short distance, but owing to the dense fog returned back to our anchorage. To-day we buried one of our men, Robert King, Quartermaster, who had been lying ill for some days. From our anchorage we could see a range of high cliffs, and a small village known as Warrenton. Thinking that there might be batteries erected there, it was decided upon to go up and introduce ourselves by way of informing Mr. Secesh that we are still on the lookout for them. At five P. M., got under way again in company of the *Albatross*. Steamed up, and when in good range opened fire; continued on up until we had passed by the cliffs, where we expected to find guns mounted, but there were none to be found or at least no response was made to our firing. At six thirty, P. M., came to anchor about three miles above Warrenton. We are now lying about six or seven miles below Vicksburg, and can see the city quite distinctly. This has been quite an adventurous week to us.

March 22d. At ten A. M., the *Albatross* got under way and dropped down the river a short distance, and shelled the batteries at Warrenton, receiving in return a brisk fire from musketry and field pieces; after engaging the batteries a short time, came up and anchored ahead of us. Last night a very large coal lighter was floated down to us from the fleet above Vicksburg, the enemy not discovering it until it had got some distance below their batteries, at which time they fired a few shots at it, but doing it no damage. We are not altogether out of coal, but as it is believed that we are in rather a tight fix, it has been deemed necessary to take in a good supply of this precious article. To-day the ship's company have been engaged coaling ship from lighter. The *Albatross* is also taking in coal from the same lighter.

March 26th. At ten A. M., beat to quarters, and loaded port battery with 10-sec. shell. At eleven fifteen hove up port anchor, beat to general quarters, and steamed down past Warrenton, firing our port battery into the enemy's casemates, but received no return. Came to anchor below Warrenton. Weather still stormy.

March 24th. Everything continues quiet. This afternoon it cleared up, and the sun made its appearance once more, which made things in general assume a more lively appearance. To-night we are expecting one or two boats down from the upper fleet. I think that if they succeed in passing by the batteries at Vicksburg they will be very fortunate, as it is almost a matter of impossibility for a vessel to pass their casemates without being sunk, or at least very materially damaged; however, it is very probable that an attempt will be made, as it is highly necessary that we should have some assistance with us, in order to succeed in our object here. Our men have been engaged to-day erecting a barricade of sails on port side of poop deck; also building a breastwork of hammocks around the wheel.

March 25th. This morning, at five thirty, heard heavy firing up the river in the direction of Vicksburg, which continued until six A. M., at which time we got under way and steamed up the river, beat to quarters, and shelled the rebel earthworks at Warrenton. The rebels returned our fire with rifled field pieces and musketry. At seven fifteen A. M., passed the batteries and discovered ahead the U. S. ram *Switzerland* and *Lancaster*, both having just passed the batteries at Vicksburg. The former vessel received a shot through one of her boilers, and the latter sunk from injuries received in the action. Three of the *Switzerland's* men were very badly scalded; the crew of the *Lancaster* were all saved. At seven thirty A. M. brought ship to anchor above Warrenton. This afternoon Mr. Gabaudan, the Admiral's Secretary, returned.

March 26th. To-day the men have been at work forming barricades on the poop deck and forecastle with hammocks and old sails; it will prove to be quite a protection to the men who are exposed at these points, as Minie balls are dealt out to us in a profuse manner generally.

We were honored to-day with a visit from Major-General Grant and staff. A consultation of war was held on board by them and our Admiral.

March 27th. We are still lying at our anchorage above Warrenton; everything quiet.

March 28th. This morning at four o'clock all hands were called; five A. M., got ship under way; five-thirty A. M., opened fire upon the batteries at Warrenton again; the enemy fired very few shots. Our loss is two very slightly wounded; the vessel sustained no injury except being hulled once, and the chain cable attached to lower yard arms cut in one place. Weather very fine; lay all day at anchor below Warrenton.

March 29th. Last evening at eight o'clock a severe storm set in, the wind blew very heavy; it rained, thundered and lightened exceeding anything I have ever seen before; at eleven o'clock we were obliged to let go our port anchor, as it was discovered that the ship was dragging. Half of the ship's company were kept stationed at their guns, to be ready in case of any emergency, while the balance of the men were below sleeping in their hammocks; the night was dreadful. At one A. M. an object was seen moving down the river; it was reported by the lookout forward; the rattle was immediately sprung, calling all hands to quarters; those who were below in their hammocks were suddenly aroused from their slumbers, "and such a getting up stairs you never did see." The object drifted down with the current until opposite our ship, and here it fetched up on the left bank of the river, which is, of course, the secesh side. Great excitement prevailed—the night being so very dark and stormy, it was feared that it might be one of the enemy's boats stealing its way down to make an attack upon us. It is a mistaken idea of theirs, if they think they will catch us napping; however, this mysterious object, after the elapse of half an hour or so, was made out to be a steamer of some kind. We did not fire, although every gun was primed and ready, and every lock-string held taut, only waiting for the word of command to fire, but it was not deemed necessary, and one watch was sent below to turn in, while the other watch remained on deck at their guns, keeping a bright lookout for the enemy. At three o'clock the storm cleared up, the wind was still blowing very heavily, however; at daylight, this morning, the weather was quite clear, although very chilly. By this time we were informed that the mysterious object which caused so much excitement last night, was no less than the steamer *Vicksburg*, which had been tied up to the wharf, under the batteries of Vicksburg, for a long time. It is quite evident that she broke loose from her moorings in consequence of the heavy storm which prevailed. This afternoon, two of our boats' crews were dispatched to board her; they returned, stating that she was a mere hulk, no machinery in her whatever; each of the men brought off something as a trophy, such as blankets, old boots, and a few old pictures, also half a dozen good muskets.

March 30th. To-day we have been taking in provisions that were sent down to us from the upper fleet; it was sent to us in the same manner that our coal was a few days ago—a large lighter filled, and then sent drifting down with the current at night. The gunboat *Albatross*, which is kept in readiness at all times, was notified to keep a bright lookout ahead, and when an object which answered to the appearance of a scow or lighter made its appearance, it was to steam up alongside and make fast and tow it in; in this way we receive our provisions; attempt was made by the enemy to destroy the barge while passing their batteries, but it was no go. The day has been very pleasant and clear, although quite chilly.

March 31st. This morning at six o'clock, got under way and steamed down the river, followed by the *Albatross*, and ram *Switzerland*; at eight-thirty A. M. we all came to anchor; sent boats on shore for fresh provisions; unfortunately but very little could be obtained; at six-thirty P. M. got under way again, and proceeded on down the river. Came in sight of Grand Gulf, continued on our way; beat to general quarters; at seven-thirty P. M. came within range and opened fire. The enemy replied very briskly, but we were too much for them this time, and drove them from their guns. They rallied, but were obliged to retreat the second time. Their loss must have been very great. Our loss during this action was one man mortally wounded. This was one of the sharpest fights we have yet had. After the action was over and the ship brought to anchor for the night, all hands were called on the quarter-deck to splice the main brace.

Jones, who was wounded to-day, deserves more than a passing notice. He was a fine young man, and dearly beloved by his shipmates. He was wounded by a bolt from a stanchion, which passed entirely through his body while he was in the act of carrying a shell to his gun. With the bolt in his body he tried to lift the projectile, but his strength failed him and he went below to the surgeon to have his wound dressed. The doctor could not get it out, and poor Jones suffered all night. He was a brave man, and will die regretted by our officers and men.

April 1st. This morning at five o'clock, William Jones, seaman, who was wounded during the action at Grand Gulf last night, departed this life. At six A. M. weighed and started on down the river; at eleven-fifteen A. M. passed Natchez; at two-thirty P. M. came in sight of Ellis's Cliffs, beat to general quarters; it was expected we would meet with some opposition, but nothing of a hostile nature occurred; at five P. M. came in sight of Port Adams, beat to quarters as usual, but met with no opposition; both of the above places are most excellent situations for batteries; at six-thirty P. M. arrived at the mouth of Red River; here we brought our fleet to anchor for the night. It will be remembered that our fleet at present consists of three vessels, namely: the *Hartford*, gunboat *Albatross*, and ram *Switzerland*: whereas at one time we could muster about thirty-seven or eight, including the mortar vessels. The contrast is quite impressive to those who are personally interested in the welfare of things on the Mississippi.

April 2nd. We are still lying quietly at our anchorage at the mouth of Red River; weather quite warm.

April 4th. The day has been spent in making arrangements to repel any attack that might be advanced by the enemy at night, by way of putting up boarding nettings, &c. It is rumored that the enemy intends boarding our ship with a large force; if such an attempt should be made, they will find that they have something more than the *Harriet Lane* to deal with. If the attempt is made, it is my humble opinion that it will only be the means of increasing our present fleet to a somewhat larger number than what it is at present. This afternoon, the *Albatross* steamed up the river a few miles, reconnoitering; after being absent three or four hours, returned with the cheering intelligence that fresh beef was the order of the day. We were provided with an allowance of fresh pork, beef, chickens, &c., which was very acceptable to all hands. Nothing further has occurred worthy of note. The day has been very warm.

April 5. This is the holy Sabbath day. Between the hours of nine and ten A. M., inspected crew at quarters, after which all hands were called to muster. Performed Divine service, and mustered crew around capstan. Warm and pleasant weather.

April 6th. At four thirty A. M., weighed anchor and steamed down the river, arriving off Bayou Sara, which is about forty-eight miles below the mouth of Red River. Came to anchor and sent two boats on shore in charge of officers, the crews of which were armed, for the purpose of destroying some ten thousand bushels of corn meal and sweet potatoes found piled upon the levee, which had been transported by rebel steamers down the river, and landed there for transportation to the Confederate army at Port Hudson, as we afterwards learned from conversation with the inhabitants of this village, who flocked around us while we were employed making way with it. Every bag, except what we thought proper to take on board the ship for the officers' and men's consumption, was thrown into the muddy Mississippi. The villagers thought it hard to destroy this property in this manner, since they had to pay so high for it; but we, not wishing to have it reach the enemy, could not see it in this light. Before finishing this, let me remark that Bayou Sara was once a very handsome spot, but last year guerillas invested it and fired upon our transports, and the iron-clad *Essex* opened upon the place and laid it in ruins. A few frame buildings and the walls of some brick ones only remain to tell its fate. The remains of these buildings look to the observer like the ruins of some ancient castles in the old world, and the artist might here find a good subject for his pencil and canvas.

At one thirty P. M. got under way again, continuing on our trip down the river until within five miles of Port Hudson, when we turned around and came to anchor. From our anchorage the rebel batteries at Port Hudson, are visible to the eye, and many an officer and blue jacket has remarked that he cannot conceive how we ever stood the concentrated fire of and passed those batteries with so little loss of life and injury to ship, on the night of ever-memorable 14th of March last.

April 7th. This afternoon some men were seen on shore making signals with a flag. Thinking it to be some parties from the lower fleet wishing to communicate with us, we ordered our army signal officer to exchange signals with them, but he found that it was impossible to do so, as they used different signals from ours. The gunboat *Albatross* then got under way, and found them to be some of the enemy, and shelled them off.

Between eight and nine o'clock, P. M., as near as I can recollect, we fired three guns at intervals of three minutes each, and sent up three rockets with same intervals intervening, to attract the attention of lower fleet, but received no answer to same. Mr. Gabaudan, the Admiral's Secretary, with despatches, left the ship in a skiff to run the gauntlet of the rebel batteries, taking with him a contraband for oarsman, to communicate with the vessels below. Another skiff with two contrabands in it was sent away from the ship about the same time as the one first mentioned, for the purpose of distracting the attention of the emeny's pickets from the other boat, or in case either were discovered, to give one a chance to escape. About ten o'clock P. M., a rocket was observed sent up from below, as a signal from the lower fleet that the experiment had proved a success.

April 8th. At five A. M., got under way and steamed up the river; at eight forty came to anchor three miles above Bayou Sara, opposite a large plantation; among other objects a saw-mill was here seen in operation; sent a boat on shore in charge of an officer and an armed crew for the purpose of foraging; after capturing a quantity of sheep they returned on board; at four thirty P. M., got under way again, and continued on our way up the river; at seven P. M., brought ship to anchor for the night near Texas landing.

April 9th. At six A. M., got up anchor and steamed up the river; at eleven A. M., two rebel steamers were discovered ahead of us near the mouth of Red River (one of which was of large proportions), and approaching same with the intention of entering it They no doubt had in our absence come out of Red River and transported a mail and provisions to the Confederate army at Vicksburg, and were now returning, having accomplished their work; as soon as we were discovered by them, they everlastingly did get up and keep putting on a full head of steam to escape capture by the "infernal Yanks," as they called us. The larger steamer of the two was successful in her effort to escape, but the other was bagged by us, a shot from our Sawyer rifle hitting her, or passing so near to the heads of those on board that they brought up with their craft among the bushes, and commenced blowing the steam whistle of same for assistance from the other, which was by this time well up Red River, her smoke only being visible to us from outside. Some of her crew made their escape, I believe, by taking to the bushes, when they saw that their cry for help was of no avail. Since we had come to an anchor off the mouth of Red River, in the Mississippi, and this steamer was just a few yards up first-mentioned stream, around a point of land. We sent the *Albatross*, our tender (a light draught gunboat), after our prize; she was successful in her mission, and soon returned with a miniature paddle-wheel boat, by name the *J. D. Clarke*, and brought her alongside of us.

The *Albatross* brought also three prisoners on board of us from off the rebel steamer,—one a secesh major, another an engineer, and the third party a fireman of the boat. This afternoon the Admiral paroled two of the above-mentioned parties, the engineer and fireman, and retained the major.

We are at anchor off the mouth of Red River, with logs on the ship's side, about where the boilers and machinery are situated, as a protection against injury from rebel rams, should they be so pugnacious as to come out of Red River some dark night and try their butting powers.

April 10th. This morning we got under way and steamed down the river a short distance, where we came to an anchor, and sent boats with boatswain and armed crews on shore to procure logs for ships' side. They returned with several large ones for that purpose, and also some hogs they had shot in the bushes for their own consumption.

While at anchor here, according to orders previously given two of our engineers, with a working party composed of firemen and coal heavers, after removing boilers and machinery and all articles of value, went to work with hammers, axes, &c., demolishing our fairy boat and prize *J. D. Clarke* and sending her hull to the bottom of the Mississippi by means of scuttling. Weather exceedingly warm and calm. Returned during this P. M. to our anchorage off mouth of Red River.

April 11th. Everything quiet to-day. During the afternoon, the *Albatross* (our chicken, as the boys now call her) returned from a reconnoitering expedition up to Fort Adams, for the purpose of ascertaining whether or not the rebels were fortifying that place. I understand she ascertained that they were not, although contrabands coming on board of us from that vicinity, inform us that they were. This is not the first instance that these negroes have told similar lies to us, and made us a good deal of trouble for nothing. Every day we receive reinforcements to the already large number of contrabands we now have to feed, and soon I expect we will be able to form a regiment, composed of these runaways, and send them wherever their services may be required. They are more an encumbrance than an article of use on board a man-of-war, and for my part I wish we were rid of them. In other words, they are a nuisance not to be tolerated (I hope) long in the U. S. Navy. We have some specimens of dark ebony who have been on board the ship a few seconds over a week or ten days, and a white man cannot speak to one of them and receive a civil answer. One cause, and the principal one, of all this is, if my experience teaches me anything, that every officer and man on board any of our vessels, do not all treat them alike. But enough has been said by me about this race of benighted beings. I will leave them here, after remarking that I pity them because they have not good sense, for if they had they would never leave a plantation (a good home during their whole life, and a kind master,) to cast themselves adrift upon strangers and a cold, unfeeling world. I know many will, and I dare say do now, wish themselves back from whence they were foolish enough to run away.

April 12th. Lying off mouth of Red River; at ten A. M. inspected ship and crew, and half an hour afterwards, performed Divine service on quarter-deck. Nothing more worthy of note occurred during the remainder of these twenty-four hours, except that at 10 o'clock P. M. a sudden alarm was given, caused by a lookout hearing a bell tolled on shore, and reported it to be that of a steamer coming out of Red River; the rattle was sprung, calling all hands to quarters. The men turned out of their hammocks, got them up on deck and stowed in the hammock nettings, and were at their guns, ready for action, in five minutes after the alarm was given. It proved to be a false alarm, and one watch went below and turned in on the soft side of a plank.

April 13th. Commences with pleasant weather, and continued so during the early hours, nothing of importance occurring. At seven thirty P. M., heavy squalls of rain came on, accompanied by thunder and lightning. The storm raged up to midnight. Since no awnings or boom covers were spread, tarpaulins placed over the hatches, or allowed to be, the berth deck was a trough for the water, and caught it all; the watch below (poor lads) with no hammocks slung to turn into, or permitted to have, got no sleep; neither were their comrades on deck any more fortunate.

April 14th. Nothing has occurred or come under my notice this day worthy of especial mention. After the rain and thunder storm of last evening, the air is quite cool and agreeable—quite a relief from that of yesterday, so close, &c.

April 15th. This morning, at six o'clock, hove up anchor, and steamed down the river; at ten o'clock, brought ship to anchor five miles above Port Hudson, for the purpose of communicating from masthead, by army signals, with vessels of lower fleet; signalizing from masthead, during the day, with U. S. sloop-of-war *Richmond.* At six o'clock, Mr. Gabaudan, Admiral's Secretary, returned on board, in company with some army officers, across the point of land, from lower fleet, after an absence of seven days, upon business of great importance with Major-General Banks at New Orleans. He brought cheering army news. Gen. Augur, with a large force of Banks's men, was in the rear of Port Hudson, cutting off their possibility of receiving supplies from that quarter, while we had blockaded the mouth of Red River, keeping them from transporting any provisions or stores from Texas out of this stream, and thence down the Mississippi; so the reader must admit that, unless they have a large quantity of beeves and provisions, this rebel stronghold must soon surrender to our arms. Starvation, when it begins, will do the work, which will be better than our being hasty, fighting, and losing thousands of valuable lives.

April 16th. Mr. Eaton, of U. S. A. Signal Corps, receiving despatches from and transmitting despatches to U. S. S. *Richmond*, by means of signals from main-masthead. *Albatross* engaged shelling the woods on the point opposite Port Hudson, where rebel pickets were stationed—our mail matter being on its way overland, in charge of an officer and some of the crew of the *Richmond*, at this time. At three P. M. our mail arrived, and the *Albatross's* boat fetched it on board of us, returning again with the party who brought it over to us, renewing her shelling of the woods while it was returning below again. These carriers of the United State mail (overland), while in the performance of their duty this day, were fired at by rebel bushwhackers, chased, and came near being captured by same, before reaching the river's edge and coming under the protection of our guns.

At five P. M., up anchor, got under way, and stood up the river a little farther; at seven thirty P. M., came to anchor a short distance above the village of Bayou Sara, opposite a large and splendid plantation, upon which, and but a few yards from the river's bank, with fine shade trees in front and rear, loomed up a fine planter's residence, and, adjoining same, an overseer's humble cottage, near which were the quarters for the hands employed on the place.

April 7th. Commences with warm and pleasant weather. At five-thirty A. M., called all hands, and hove up anchor; got under way, and were once more stemming the current of the Mississippi, which is none other than a four-knot one, by the way. In many instances the residences of the rich and affluent planters or merchants looked to be deserted by the owners, and the overseer and negroes working in the fields were the only parties to be seen. What an example of the ravages of war! and how many fair ones occupy apartments in some of these dwellings, closed up, as I have said, as if they were haunted and deserted, who have a husband, father, brother, or other relative, in this war, fighting against their country, and, according as they have been made to believe by corrupt politicians and arch traitors, for their rights, their altars, and their firesides; when, if the truth were known, they had taken up arms to overthrow the best government the sun ever shone upon, and substituted a monarchy, placing bad men in power—a government for a few, not for a whole. How men can, in this enlighted age, become so deluded, is a wonder.

April 18th. Warm weather; nothing worthy of mention has occurred during these twenty-four hours; at anchor off mouth of Red River. Col. Ackelon's plantation and residence a little distance ahead of us on the left bank of the river; it is a beautiful place; the Colonel I believe to be a good Union man; the Admiral's, Captain's, and ward room and forward officer's table are supplied with the fruits and vegetables of the season, grown upon his place. I believe he has five inland plantations, making, with the one fronting upon the river, six, and is very wealthy; he owns at least one thousand negroes; he is afflicted with the gout; is a man in the prime of life, and a cripple; he owns a beautiful mansion in Nashville, Tenn., which his wife is living in at present; our officers have often gone ashore and dined with him, and he has been on board and paid his respects to Admiral Farragut and Commodore Palmer several times; he has also been so kind as to allow us to bury some of our men who have been so unfortunate as to get killed by the enemy, or die of fever contracted in this southern clime.

April 19th. This morning the ram *Switzerland* and gunboat *Albatross*, got under way and entered the mouth of Red River, with the intention of proceeding a short distance up same, to find the enemy if possible. In the afternoon however, they returned from their reconnoissance, having seen nothing of him. It seems rather singular after all his boasting of what he was going to do—come down from Alexandria some night, with his ram the *Queen of the West* (a vessel captured from Col. Ellet, some time since), the *Dr. Beatty*, and some other steamers, and try their butting power upon us, and if not able to punch a hole into the old *Hartford* and sink her where she lies anchored, then make her skedaddle, and chase here down the river until she came under the guns of Port Hudson, when her destruction would be sure. Secesh is a great blower, and as the story goes, a barking dog never bites, so we must not fear him. He has had many propitious nights to put his threats into execution, and his failure to do so prove him a braggart and a liar of the basest kind.

April 20th. Still lying to an anchor off the mouth of Red River. The ram *Switzerland*, Commander Col. Ellet, and *Albatross*, Lieut.-Commander Hart, at anchor ahead of us, close in shore. Let me here remark, before going any further (since I think the reader is not aware of the fact), that the crew stand watch and watch every night at their guns. They are allowed to lie down on deck between same, and go to sleep. This is a necessary precaution against a surprise, and to have the men near at hand should the enemy be so foolish as to attack us where we are. We were also expecting daily to hear of Gen. Banks, who had gone around by way of Brashear City, from New Orleans to Alexandria, capturing and taking possession of same, and of seeing some of his transports some night, coming down and out of Red River. Warm and pleasant weather. All quiet on the Rappahannock—(I mean on the Mississippi.)

April 21st. Very rainy weather. Everything dark and cloudy overhead, and the faces of the ship's company bearing anything but a smile upon them. A heavy pressure seems to be weighing down their hearts—something more than common must be the cause of this depression of spirits. A sailor does not have the blues often, and when he does, something extraordinary is the cause of it. Jack is full of fight, and when he cannot fight his enemy, he will get in a quarrel with his own friends and shipmates. Secesh will not give Jack a chance to show his powers of endurance, and he is sick at heart, and says he *wants to go home.*

April 22d. Commences with cool, pleasant weather. Crew employed painting ship, &c. Our color has always been black, but owing to a late order from the Department, at Washington, all vessels composing the Western Gulf Squadron are now to be painted a lead color, which is hardly distinguishable from the water of the Mississippi.

April 23d. At six A. M. weighed anchor, got under way, and steamed down the river, *Albatross* and ram *Switzerland* in company, bringing up the rear. On our way down came to several times, for the purpose of destroying some flat boats which we came across in the river, and which were used in the transportation of sugar, molasses, &c., across the river to the rebel forces at Port Hudson. At two P. M. brought ship to anchor, five miles above the batteries at Port Hudson. Engaged signalizing (by means of army signals) from masthead to lower fleet.

April 24th. Commences with pleasant, warm weather. This afternoon, signalizing to vessels of lower fleet. Received a mail from sloop-of-war *Richmond* during the day, across the point of land, which separated us from vessels of our fleet below, and which gladdened the hearts of many, or of all those who were so fortunate as to receive a letter from home and friends most dear. At five P. M. hove up anchor again, and steamed up river. At seven P. M. brought ship to anchor a short distance above Bayou Sara. *Albatross* and ram *Switzerland* anchored astern.

April 25th. At five A. M., hove up anchor and continued on our way up the river, now and then coming to for the purpose of destroying flat-boats and sugar manufactories which were supplying the rebels with sugar and molasses whenever we were not bobbing around in the vicinity. Their cake is now all dough, since hereafter we will have one or two steamers patroling the river all the time. At two o'clock, P. M., brought ship to anchor off the mouth of Red River, *Albatross* and ram *Switzerland* making fast ahead inshore.

April 26th. Commenced with rainy weather, continuing stormy until eight o'clock, A. M., when it cleared off, the sun shining from out of the clouds in all its glory. The rain had cooled and purified the atmosphere to a very pleasant degree, and all enjoyed the change. At ten thirty A. M., called all hands to muster, and performed Divine service on the quarter-deck. As yet no attempt has been made by the enemy to attack us, and I am disposed to believe he has decided under the circumstances that discretion is the better part of valor.

April 27th. All still on the river; very stormy weather.

April 28th. Commences with pleasant weather; during this morning the *Albatross* and *Switzerland* got under way and entered the mouth of Red River, going up that stream a short distance on a reconnoissance; returned during the afternoon without having seen the enemy, or any batteries erected by him to prove that he was in the vicinity. A rumor is afloat to-day among the ship's company that Charleston has lately been attacked by our army and naval forces and captured. We have nothing definite, though, in regard to the truth of such report; still it has its believers, and they are much excited over it. I have no doubt but that ere long we will have something happen that will cause more excitement and rejoicing than the fall of Charleston; I mean the surrender of Vicksburg and Port Hudson. The weather is cool and pleasant, the rain of yesterday having purified the atmosphere to a great extent.

April 29th. Commences with pleasant weather. Nothing of importance has occurred this twenty-four hours.

April 30th. We have information, through Col. Ackelon, I believe, that a battle has been fought to-day at Grand Gulf, between our naval forces under Rear-Admiral Porter, and the rebels, in which we lost one of our gunboats, but were successful in driving the enemy out of some of their batteries and silencing some of their guns. We have hopes that by the landing of some of Gen. Grant's men a short distance above and in the rear of Grand Gulf, and storming same, that it has been taken possession of ere this. The prospects of the

Mississippi river soon being clear of obstructions are brightening every day.

May 1st. The first day of May commences with clear and pleasant weather. This afternoon the Admiral despatched the ram *Switzerland* up the river as far as Grand Gulf, for news of what was going on in that quarter. At nine o'clock this evening, a rocket was reported as seen sent up Red River, and soon after a steamer's light was seen coming down. Immediately the rattle was sprung, giving the alarm, and a few minutes afterwards all hands were at their guns and stations, while nearly all, officers and men, believed it was one of our own transports from Brashear City, via Berwick's Bay and Atchafalaya River; still, they might be mistaken, and it was proper to be prepared against a surprise should it prove to be the enemy. Soon the vessel made her appearance, coming out of Red River, and signalized, by means of different colored lights, her number. Had she been a little dilatory in doing so, I have no doubt but a fight would have been the upshot of the matter, since the men were all anxious for the fray, and ready, with fifteen broadside guns, twelve of them nine-inch, bearing on their target, and only waiting for the old hero, the Admiral, to give them the order. She proved to be the U. S. gunboat and transport *Arizona*. Upon our hailing her and asking in trumpet voice what steamer that was, all was excitement unbounded among officers and crew, and a few moments of stillness and suspense followed ere she returned an answer to our inquiry; when her answer was known, joy pervaded the hearts of all; three cheers were heartily given, the retreat beat, and every one left his quarters, thanking Him whose sun is made to shine upon the just and the unjust, that such success had crowned our efforts, and communication through another channel with our army, and New Orleans was now open to us, by the arrival of this long-expected visitor and stranger. The *Arizona* came to off our starboard quarter, and sent a boat with her Captain in same on board of us, with despatches from General Banks to Admiral Farragut; after communicating with us, she wended her way back again, *via* Red and Atchafalaya Rivers to Brashear City.

Jeff has had the laugh on us for a long time, but now the tables are turned, and we come in to relieve him and take a spell at this pleasant recreation. I wonder how he likes it? Any how, we can now say, "Jeff, as you like it; this is kind of hard treatment of you, showing that we d——d Yankees have very little respect for your feelings; we know how arduously you have served your constituents, and that you need some rest. It shall not be denied you, and we shall take sole charge of affairs on the Mississippi, likewise Red River, until Port Hudson and Vicksburg fall."

May 2d. Commences with clear and pleasant weather. Nothing occurred worthy of mention during nearly the entire day, the regular routine of naval discipline being gone through with on this day as upon all other days; at eight thirty o'clock, P. M., lights seen up Red River and reported from lookouts at mast-head; beat to quarters, and got ship ready for action. In a short time they made their appearance coming out of Red River, signalizing to us by different colored lights; as soon as they came within hailing distance, hailed them; they gave us to understand that they were respectively the U. S. gunboats *Arizona* and *Estrella* from Brashear City; they steamed on ahead of us, and anchored close in shore.

May 3d. Commences with clear and pleasant weather; inspected crew at quarters, and performed Divine service at ten o'clock, this morning, on quarter-deck. While at service the gunboats *Albatross*, *Estrella*, and *Arizona* got under way and started up Red river on a reconnoissance,—the little *Albatross* taking the lead.

May 4th. Commences with clear and pleasant weather; at one-thirty A. M., lights reported coming down the Mississippi river; the rattle was sprung, calling crew to quarters; soon however, signals were exchanged between us and the approaching vessels, each vessel making her number by means of displaying different colored lights, by means of which we ascertained their names. They proved to be a portion of Rear-Admiral Porter's fleet of iron-clads, having but lately run the gauntlet of the Vicksburg batteries, under a tremendous fire from the enemy, and still later engaged the rebel fortifications at Grand Gulf, and with the aid of some of our forces under General Grant drove the rebels out of the same, making many prisoners and taking possession of the place; as they passed on down and rounded our stern, the excitement on board the old sea-dog *Hartford* was more than I can describe. These western iron-clads are very queer looking specimens of river craft. The above-noticed iron-clads and gunboats proved to be the *Benton*, (Flag-ship of Rear-Admiral Porter), *Pittsburgh, LaFayette*, ram *General Sterling Price*, and tug-boat *Ivy*; the ram *Switzerland* accompanied them down.

The *Ivy*, tender to the *Benton*, came alongside of us, and Rear-Admiral D. D. Porter came on board to communicate with Admiral Farragut. Clear and pleasant, but rather warm weather; all the forenoon of this day employed supplying iron-clads *Benton* and *Pittsburgh*, and *LaFayette* with ammunition; received a mail on board; at three P. M., Admiral Porter's fleet of vessels, with him in charge, got under way, rounded our stern, and entered the mouth of Red river, ram *Switzerland* taking the lead, intending before returning to clear out this stream of all obstructions placed in the way of the free navigation of same by the rebels, and accomplish the capture of Alexandria; at four P. M., the gunboat *Albatross* returned from reconnoissance up Red river; she anchored ahead of us; her Captain came on board with the information that they had had a fight in the morning with the rebels, a short distance from the mouth of the river, at a battery called Fort De Russy, and had two men killed in the action, which lasted about an hour, and had her wheel shot away; one of the parties killed was a Mr. Hamilton, a pilot of this ship. The *Albatross* was successful in putting a shot through the boilers of a rebel steamboat, from which an explosion took place, and a large number of the enemy were scalded beyond recovery, their awful cries of agony and for help pierced the hearts of many of the brave tars on board the *Albatross*, causing a feeling of sympathy for the poor fellows. The *Albatross*, I must not omit to say in closing this, could not get nearer to this battery than five hundred yards, on account of a barrier or raft of logs obstructing the navigation of the river at this place, constructed by the rebels. About five P. M., Mr. J. Hamilton's body was received on board from gunboat *Albatross*; also the steering wheel of same vessel in a badly damaged condition; and I will here remark the shot which struck this wheel knocked over a bale or more of cotton, which was used as a barricade around it, upon our pilot, causing such injuries internally that he died therefrom.

May 5th. Commences with a sky overcast and cloudy, and thunder and lightning, precursors of a storm; finished repairing *Albatross's* wheel broken in action of 4th inst.; at three A. M., at daylight, sent a party on shore to dig a grave; at five fifteen sent the body of Mr. Hamilton, pilot, on shore, in charge of Lieut. Watson, for interment; the grave was dug on the left bank of the river, a short distance below Col. Ackelon's house; at eight A. M., got under way, and steamed down the river, *Albatross* and *Sachem* in company with us; at eleven o'clock saw a flat boat ahead crossing the river opposite Bayou Sara, having two hogsheads of sugar on board; called one gun's crew to quarters, and fired the Sawyer rifle on forecastle ahead of same to bring it to, and sent the second cutter in charge of an officer and an armed crew to take it in tow; took her in tow, and brought her alongside of us and made her fast: received a white man and boy, and several negroes, prisoners from off the scow, on board; at eleven forty-five called all hands to bring ship to anchor; at twelve, noon, came to anchor five miles above Port Hudson; at one P. M., the *Albatross* and *Sachem* engaged shelling the woods on the point opposite Port Hudson, and in burning two frame buildings used by rebel pickets. Making signals from masthead to U. S. sloop-of-war *Richmond*, and receiving answers from her to same; paroled the two white prisoners; received no mail this time from lower fleet.

May 6th. Commences with clear and pleasant weather, and light breezes from the northward and westward; at six thirty-five A. M., the steamer *Sachem* got under way and steamed up the river, exchanging signals with lower fleet from mast-head; at eight forty-five called all hands up anchor, got under way, and proceeded up the river; at eleven thirty came to anchor off Point Coupée; sent forth cutter, in charge of an officer, and with six marines and an armed boat's crew, to destroy some Confederate property; at one thirty P. M., under way steaming up the Mississippi; at 3 o'clock passed the *Sachem*; at seven o'clock came to anchor off the mouth of Red river; *Albatross* also came up and anchored.

May 7th. Commences with pleasant weather; at six forty-five A. M., sent the *Albatross* down the river in search of the *Sachem*; at 9 A. M., inspected crew at quarters; at two P. M., the *Albatross* came up the river and made fast inshore ahead of us; at two forty P. M., the *Sachem* came up the river and anchored.

May 8th. Lying to an anchor in the Mississippi off the mouth of Red river; all quiet on the "Father of Waters," up to four A. M., when a scene of great excitement occurred on board of the Flag-ship *Hartford*. The reader may ask what was the cause of it? Was the enemy near? No; but our friends were, and about bidding us, maybe, a long adieu, and leaving the good old ship for other parts; and they were our best of friends,—those who had left their wives and children, homes, relations, all that tends to make home dear, to be with us, and by their presence, kind words, and noble example, encourage us to deeds of noble daring; and well, dear reader, have they performed this duty, as the preceding pages of this book will testify, having been under their command in nine general engagements with the enemy, and have come out of all victorious, with little loss of life or limb, and the least damage to ship, while other vessels of the fleet had to succumb to the destructiveness of the enemy's shot and shell, losing many valuable lives. This will appear more wonderful when it is taken into consideration that we always took the lead; we never asked others to go where we were afraid to go ourselves, and by this course of proceeding the *Hartford* has earned herself and brave Commander a name and fame at home and abroad. The rebels upon the banks of the Mississippi call her the black devil, and honorably acknowledge him who flies his broad blue pennant in defiance to them from her masthead, to be a bold, brave, and daring old warrior. I think it is a well-deserved compliment to the old naval hero, who never knew what fear or defeat was, and also to the staunch and noble old vessel whose decks he has trod with such a courageous tread and quiet mien, while guiding her movements when engaged with the enemy at close quarters, and running the gauntlet of their terrible batteries under a storm of iron hail. Success to him and his brave companions in all their future operations is the wish of the writer of these few lines, and may he be spared many years yet to brighten the page of history with an account of his glorious deeds in the service of his country. Although rumored the day previous, the ship's company could not be made to believe that we were going to lose one who held such a place in the hearts of all, and had become so dear—whose name was a household one; but alas! the dawn of this day proved the rumor too true, and many a countenance of these tars, tried by fire and water, every one a hero and able to relate an account of his hair-breath escapes from the enemy, was darkened and clouded over from the effect of this sad news; others' eyes were wet with the tears they would fain conceal, but could not; their grief would find vent through this channel. All things being in readiness, at four, forty this morning, precisely, the following officers left the ship, viz . Rear-Admiral D. G. Farragut, Fleet Captain T. A. Jenkins, Fleet Surgeon J. M. Foltz, Rear-Admiral's Secretary, E. C. Gabaudan, Fleet Captain's Clerk, E. A. Palmer; also Lieut. Eaton of U. S. A. Signal Corps, and two soldiers of same; at five A. M., the *Sachem* got under way with them on board, when the lads manned the rigging, and gave three times three with a will; such cheers were seldom given by our noble sailors to any person or persons, and the honored recipients of same will long remember the event.

May 9th. At nine A. M., inspected crew at quarters; *Albatross* under way at ten A. M., steaming up the river; at four P. M., the *Albatross* returned from up the river and anchored ahead of us; at ten thirty P. M., heard very heavy firing from the southward and eastward; heard the last report at eleven twenty.

May 10th. Commenced with pleasant and clear weather, which continued until six fifteen; at ten A. M., called all hands to muster, and read a general order from Rear-Admiral D. G. Farragut, after which performed Divine service; nothing more worthy of note occurred during the remainder of this day, except it be that firing of great guns was again heard down the river, at eleven fifty-five P. M., supposed to be the lower fleet bombarding the rebel batteries at Port Hudson.

May 11th. Is ushered upon us with pleasant weather, and light breezes from south-east. From noon to 1 o'clock, A. M., heavy firing heard down the river; at five fifty U. S. steamer *Estrella* came down Red river from Alexandria, with despatches to Commodore Palmer; at six forty-five the Albatross got under way and stood up the river; sent our pilot, Mr. Carroll, on board of her; at nine o'clock inspected crew at quarters, employed placing logs on port side of ship to protect the boilers and machinery against assaults from the enemy's rams or iron-clad boats; *Albatross* came down the river and anchored in her old berth; at noon, a tug came down from upper fleet, Porter's, with despatches and a mail; at one P. M., the gunboat *Estrella* got under way and entered the mouth of Red river on her return to Alexandria; at one thirty the tug-boat followed her, steaming away very fast; at three o'clock the steam tug and tender to the ship *Benton* came down and out of Red river, having Rear-Admiral Porter on board, and came alongside of us; Admiral Porter came on board of us and communicated with the Commodore. These are all the important occurrences of this day, also all the arrivals and departures of vessels at this station.

May 12th. This morning, at 1 o'clock, heard heavy firing down the river in the neighborhood of Port Hudson, which ceased in twenty minutes afterwards; at five forty-five steamer *L. A. Sykes* arrived from Alexandria, and at six thirty steamed back up Red river again; finished tricing the logs upon port side of ship; at 3 P. M., the steamer *General Price* came down Red river; light, easterly breezes; at four twenty the ironclad gunboat *Pittsburgh*, from Black river, came down and anchored ahead of us; ten of our men, volunteers who went on the expedition up Red river on board of her, returned to this ship with bag and hammock; at seven thirty-five the iron-clad *Benton*, flag-ship of Rear-Admiral Porter's fleet, came down and out of Red river also; sent steam tug *Ivy* for our men, some twenty in number, detached on board of her for above referred-to expedition; the lads returned in good spirits, having had a pleasant trip to Alexandria and back, which place is now occupied by General Banks's forces, and has the glorious stars and stripes once more flung to the breeze, whose colors the inhabitants are thrice glad to see once more. The boats did not come across the enemy during their absence. Many of the beautiful plantations of noted secessionists on Red river, left in charge of overseers, furnished the boys plenty of good food, such as chickens, turkeys, eggs, &c., and greatly did they enjoy this change of fodder from hard bread and salt horse.

May 13th. Commences with pleasant weather; firing commenced between the hours of one and two o'clock this morning, and continued up to three o'clock; it was heard to the southward; at daylight the gunboat *Benton*, with the General *Price* and tug *Ivy*, got under way and steamed up the river; at 10 o'clock a steam tug came down and out of Red river alongside of us, with despatches for Rear-Admiral D. D. Porter; gave her some coal; at two P. M., after finished coaling, the tug got under way and steamed up the Mississippi river in chase of the flag-ship *Benton*, and I think she was not long in overhauling this slow, cumbersome, and ungainly specimen of river craft. This afternoon the *Albatross* got under way and steamed up Red river; at six o'clock *Albatross* returned from her foraging trip up Red river; received from her a quantity of fresh beef.

May 14th. Commences, "for a change," with stormy weather, squalls of rain, and continued so during forenoon of this day; at seven A. M. the despatch steamer *L. A. Sykes* came out of Red River, direct from Alexandria, and made fast alongside of us, bringing despatches from Gen. Banks to Commodore Palmer; also the gunboat *Sachem* arrived; at seven thirty the *Sykes* got under way and went up Red river. This is a fine and fast little steamer, and is of great service to us; at six forty five P. M. the U. S. steames *Arizonr* came down and out of Red River, with Brig.-Gen. Dwight as a passenger, on his way to Grand Gulf to take command of some of Gen. Banks's forces there. He came on board and paid his respects to Commodore Palmer. Let me here remark that this gentleman and soldier but a short time since had a brother killed near Alexandria by some guerrillas, while in the performance of his duty, whose loss he feels very much. He was a Captain in the army, and at the time he was killed was carrying despatches from Gen. Banks to some part of his command, and was mounted, but unarmed; at seven P. M. the *Arizona* steamed on her way up the river, bound to Grand Gulf. Nothing more of importance occurred during the remainder of these twenty-four hours.

May 15th. At eight forty A. M. the iron-clad *Lafayette* made her appearance, coming down Red river; she soon came out of same into the great Mississippi, and communicated with us. Between the hours of twelve and four o'clock P. M., picked up out of the Mississippi, which came down from above, supposed to have been thrown overboard by some gunboat steamer, sixteen bales of cotton, in the production of which Dixie is famous.

May 16th. Commences with light southerly breezes; at seven A. M. saw a wreck floating down, and sent the gunboat *Sachem* to see what it was; at nine A. M. inspected crew at quarters. The supposed wreck proved to be a snag;at 10 A.M., Commodore Palmer, and his clerk Nathaniel P. S. Thomas, also the Paymaster, Mr. Wm. F. Meredith, left the ship to go on board of the steamer *Sachem*. *Sachem* got under way, and steamed up Red river. Between the hours of eight and twelve (midnight), firing was heard down the river, inland, in the direction of Port Hudson.

May 17th. Commences with calm, warm weather; at ten A. M. inspected ship and crew; and at ten thirty A. M. called all hands to muster, and performed Divine service on the quarter-deck; at four thirty P. M. the *Albatross* came down the Mississippi with a coal barge in tow, and anchored ahead of us. She had been up to Grand Gulf. The *Sachem* got under way and went up Red river. Light breezes from the northward and westward.

May 18th. At nine twenty A. M. the *Sachem* came down and out of Red river, and anchored ahead of us. The *Albatross* got under way and went down the Mississippi river. Saw the smoke of a steamer up Red river; at twelve, noon, the ram *Switzerland* came out of Red river, and communicated with us; at two P. M. the iron-clad *Pittsburgh* got under way and went down the Mississippi. Ram *Switzerland* went up Red river. A steamer reported coming down the Mississippi river; at five P. M. the ram *Gen. Sterling Price*, arrived from Vicksburg; at nine thirty P. M. ram *Switzerland* returned from a reconnoissance up Red river, having nothing, though, to report, and anchored ahead of us.

May 19th. Commences with clear and pleasant weather. Heard firing from twelve, midnight, to one A. M., in the direction of Port Hudson. From four o'clock until eight this morning, fresh easterly breezes; at five thirty A. M. steamer *Price* got under way and went up Red river, at twelve noon, the river steamer *Empire Parish*, "direct from New Orleans," came out of Red river with a coal schooner in tow, and brought same alongside of us; at one P. M. the *Empire Parish* returned up Red river; and the crew employed coaling ship remainder of the day. Received fresh beef on board.

May 20th. Another pleasant day dawns upon a sleeping world; at seven thirty A. M. finished coaling ship; have been engaged at it since yesterday at one o'clock in the afternoon, and working all night received some seventy-three or seventy-five tons on board; at ten thirty A. M. the U. S. steam ram *Gen. Price* came down and out of Red river, and communicated with us. Cast off the coal schooner and dropped her astern; at twelve M. steamer *Price* got under way and went down the Mississippi river; at three P. M. the iron-clad *Lafayette* got under way and steamed up Red river; at three forty-five P. M. the *Empire Parish* came out of Red river, and took the coal barge and schooner in tow; sent Lieut. Hall, of U. S. A. Signal Corps, and his two men on board of her, and she went up Red river; at eleven thirty P. M. the steamer *Gen. Price* came up the Mississippi river, and anchored near us. These are all the departures and arrivals of this day.

May 21st. Firing was heard before daylight, down the river; at nine A. M. the steamer *Gen. Sterling Price* got under way and went up the Mississippi river; at nine A. M. as usual, inspected the crew at quarters. Commodore James S. Palmer went up Red river in steam gunboat *Sachem*; at two P. M., and from that hour until four P. M., infantry, cavalry, and artillery, were seen passing down the left bank of the river, some of Gen. Banks's forces from the Teche country having come from Simsport or Alexandria; also two river steamers loaded with U. S. troops, came out of Red river, and made fast inshore ahead of us. Officers and men on board of them were in high spirits, knowing that it was owing to the old *Hartford's* passage of the rebel batteries at Port Hudson, on the ever-memorable night of the 14th of March last, and her effective blockade of Red river since, that they could now meet with us to-day, and be transported from here to the village of Bayou Sara, a few miles above Port Hudson, and invest the latter place, and they gratefully acknowledged the service we had done them, by giving us three rousing cheers, which our boys upon manning the rigging, returned; at four ten P. M. the steam gunboat *Estrella* came out of Red river; at five thirty P. M. the gunboat *Sachem*, with Commodore Palmer and General Banks on board, came down and out of Red river, and in twenty minutes afterwards, the steamers *Empire Parish*, *St. Maurice*, *Estrella*, *Bee*, and *Sachem*, went down the river; at seven P. M. the steamer *St. Charles*, from Red river, with a coal barge for us in tow, arrived, bringing coal vessel alongside of us, and afterwards going down the Mississippi. Heavy firing heard in the direction of Port Hudson. This is a true account of all the occurrences of this day, and as the reader will readily perceive, there have been many, and such as will be remembered by us as well as by the enemy, for a long time to come. Secesh now looks crest-fallen, and thinks the mudsills of the North have got rather the best of him; he does not see what Jeff. is about.

May 22d. At 4 o'clock this morning, got under way, and stood down the river. Let me here remark that when the boys learned, last evening, that the necessity of the blockade of Red river by us was now done away with, and that early the next morning we would heave up anchor and take our departure for an anchorage below, and somewhat nearer to the rebel batteries at Port Hudson, to aid the army in soon assaulting or storming the same, the joy and excitement among them cannot be described. I know the anchor this morning was hove up by willing hands and gladdened hearts; at five A. M. a ferry boat passed us, going down the river; at six thirty A. M. passed the steamers *St. Maurice*, *Empire Parish*, *St. Charles*, and *Bee*, made fast into the bank or levee, where they had, during the previous night or early this morning, been engaged landing infantry and artillery; at eight fifteen A. M. came to anchor off Bayou Sara. *Pittsburg, Albatross, Sachem, and Estrella*, at anchor off this place; at eight thirty A. M. steamer *Empire Parish* started up the river; at nine A. M., Gens. Banks and Andrews came on board; at ten A. M. got under way and steamed down the river; an hour afterwards anchored five miles above the batteries of Port Hudson, communicating with lower fleet by means of army signals from our mainmasthead; at five P. M. got under way, and proceeded under steam, up the river, *Albatross* in company; at five twenty P. M. it commenced to rain—the forenoon of the day, and up to this hour has been cool and pleasant in the extreme—and continued raining up to six o'clock P. M.; at six thirty P. M. arrived and came to anchor off Bayou Sara. Steam army transports *St. Maurice*, *Empire Parish*, *Gen. Banks*, and gunboat *Arizona*, came down from above, and made fast to the levee. This has been another day of excitement and work.

May 23d. Commences with pleasant weather. Two steamers came down the river about two o'clock this A. M., at three o'clock this morning, the mortar schooners below, opened a heavy fire on the batteries at Port Hudson. Between the hours of four and eight A. M. a steamer loaded with cavalry went alongside of the landing; at twelve noon, the *Arizona* went down the river, iron-clads went up the river. From eight to midnight, heavy firing heard at Port Hudson.

May 24th. Commences with pleasant weather. Light winds from S. E. Transports in sight coming down the river, and cavalry and infantry landing at the levee at Bayou Sara from four to eight A. M.; at eight thirty A. M. hove up anchor, got under way and steamed down the river; at nine thirty A. M. rounded to above Port Hudson, and fired a shell from the Sawyer rifle on poop, into the rebel batteries, to let them know we had come down to see them once more; at nine forty A. M. came to anchor five miles above Port Hudson. Received from the *Albatross* five rebel prisoners, hard looking fellows, on board, and kindly cared for them. These unfortunates were captured on a point of land opposite the rebel Gibraltar No. 2 of the Mississippi; at ten thirty A. M. called all hands to muster and performed Divine service. Heavy firing going on at Port Hudson. Received some more rebel prisoners this morning from the *Albatross*; they proved to be an officer and two privates belonging to a signal corps, they having been captured the day before by some of our pickets. Heavy firing heard in rear of Port Hudson. The mortar schooners below, engaged the rebel batteries also, from two thirty until four P. M. From four to six P. M., heavy cannonading between lower fleet and rebel batteries at Port Hudson, during this watch; also our army in rear of Port Hudson, engaged with the enemy; at six P. M. inspected crew at quarters. Received a mail on board from below.

May 25th. Commences with pleasant but warm weather. From four to eight A. M. heard musketry-firing in rear of Port Hudson. This morning Lieut. Watson went across the point to communicate with lower fleet; at eleven A. M. steamer *Bee* came down the river and communicated with us. Received on board three more rebel prisoners from the *Albatross*; at one P. M. sent fourteen rebel prisoners, in charge of Lieut. Higby, U. S. M. Corps, and fourteen marines, to Bayou Sara; the lower fleet shelling Port Hudson; at six thirty P. M. called all hands, got up anchor and steamed up river; at seven P. M. came to anchor a little further up the river. Lieut. Higby and the marines returned to the ship; at eleven forty P. M. beat to general quarters.

May 26th. Commences with pleasant weather, and only to find us engaged in shelling the woods around Port Hudson, which proved a big scare to the rebels, so much so that they deserted two fine river steamers they had concealed among the bushes upon what is called (it is a small stream) Thompson's Creek, and our pickets took possession of them; our shelling continued, at intervals, from twelve to one forty A. M., of this watch, the *Albatross* participating in it; so there was no sleep last night on board the Hartford; at four o'clock beat to general quarters again, and shelled the woods in rear of Port Hudson; mortar vessels of the lower fleet also engaged shelling the rebel works; at five thirty hove up anchor, got under way, and dropped down to our old anchorage near the port, opposite Port Hudson, and anchored; at ten o'clock sent third cutter to land Mr. Watson, who is going across the point to take our mail for the North, and despatches for the Admiral; between the hours of five and six o'clock, P. M., saw a large fire burning at Port Hudson; sent third cutter, armed, ashore for our messenger.

May 27th. At daylight this morning it was apparent to all who heard the heavy firing of artillery, and rapid discharges of musketry, that an attack had been made by our forces upon the enemy's works. The firing continued without intermission during the whole forenoon of this day. During the afternoon, occasionally heavy firing of artillery and musketry, the rebels replying at intervals with two great guns; lower fleet bombarding the rebel earthworks at Port Hudson, mortars, or bombers, as our boys call them, engaged also. A report has been circulated about the decks that during Banks's attack this morning, a battery of six guns had been captured by us, the enemy drove into their main works, and some two or three of our regiments were inside of their entrenchments.

May 28th. At three o'clock this morning hostilities commenced again between the two contending armies, with all its former ferocity, and the loud booming of cannon was in great contrast and bold relief to the low but quick mutterings of numerous volleys of musketry. The rumor of yesterday in regard to several thousand of our men being in their entrenchments we have since learned was untrue. Although the fortifications in and around Port Hudson are very formidable, and of such a nature as hard to be overcome, making this rebel stronghold almost another Gibraltar, still great confidence is put in General Banks that he will be able to surmount all these in time, and reduce the place. Admiral Farragut, on board the staunch and new sloop-of-war *Monongahela*, below Port Hudson, is aiding the army by all the means in his power towards the consummation of the reduction of this place. He has the sloops-of-war *Richmond*, *Genesee*, and iron-clad *Essex* at his command, with six mortar schooners, and I assure you he does not allow them long to remain idle, but whenever he thinks some execution can be done by the sending of a few shot or shell, grape or canister, among the rebels, they all go to work with a will to perform this duty. They are more or less engaged every day with the enemy; the rebels admit that it is not Banks they fear, but the ships, and if they were not around close to hand, Banks would have to look out for himself; without us their supplies would not be entirely cut off, and the blockade would therefore not be effective; they could not be reinforced by Kirby Smith's band of guerrillas, or some other party, by crossing the river, or cutting their way through Banks' handful of men. I give all praise, though, to Banks doing as well as he has with the forces (and quality) at his command; and although he has been repulsed, and has to fall back to his old position, in the late engagement with the Confederates, still we will not say he did not fight well and attempt to carry everything before him; but, although defeated, we look forward to the time when our arms will be successful, and that soon. Although we lost many men in these two days' fighting, yet the enemy must admit of being much cut up, and his men demoralized, which weakens him for an early renewal of hostilities.

May 29th. The cessation of hostilities on both sides seems to have, in part, taken place, and our forecastle is not crowded with officers and blue jackets, like on the two previous days, straining their eyes almost out of their sockets in their anxiety to see where our shells and those of our armies fell in the rebels' works, and what execution they do. Oh, the excitement caused by seeing two parties striving for the mastery! I presume that the almost abandonment of the siege to-day is for good reasons,—probably to rest and recover strength for an early renewal of the assault, and this time with a larger force, or else for the purpose of burying their dead, and giving the enemy an opportunity to care for theirs, the performance of which is a sacred duty, and so held by all civilized nations.

May 30th. Commences with pleasant weather. This morning, early, sent the body of Michael Walsh, marine, on shore for burial; he died at ten o'clock in the evening of yesterday, after a brief illness. During the afternoon of this day the steamer *General Price*, of upper fleet, came down from Vicksburg, bringing a mail for us, and the information that Major-General Grant is fighting hard at Vicksburg, and gaining ground; at four forty-five P. M., the *General Price* started back up the river, taking our mail; at eleven fifteen the mortar fleet below opened fire upon Port Hudson.

May 31st. At three A. M., mortar vessels below still firing upon the rebel batteries at Port Hudson; at 10 o'clock called all hands to muster on the quarter-deck, and performed Divine service; nothing of importance occurred during the remainder of this day. The weather continues pleasant, and occasional guns were heard at Port Hudson and in rear of same.

June 1st. Commences calm and pleasant; firing of musketry this morning heard at Port Hudson; in fact no day has passed since the investment of this rebel stronghold and siege of same commenced, but what more or less bombarding of it has been going on by our army and naval forces, and skirmishing with their pickets, &c.; at nine o'clock this morning inspected crew at quarters; this duty is performed every day at this hour, unless engaged in combat with the enemy, or important work is going on in the ship, calling all hands to perform their share of the labor; from eight P. M., to midnight, mortar vessels, or bombers, below, shelling the batteries at Port Hudson.

June 2d. Early this morning vessels of lower fleet fired a few shots; later, during this forenoon, sent seven rebel prisoners ashore to be taken across the point of land opposite Port Hudson to lower fleet; at nine o'clock heavy firing in rear of Port Hudson by our army; during the evening the upper batteries at Port Hudson opened fire inland.

June 3. During the early part of this day, or even the whole morning, all was quiet at Port Hudson and on the Mississippi. During early part of the afternoon the steamer *General Sterling Price* arrived from Vicksburg; fighting still going on in that quarter; at five thirty the steamer *Price* and Gen. Banks went up the river. Heard heavy cannonading going on at Port Hudson, between the two contending armies, and I am not aware as yet who's who, or who is getting the best of it; at six thirty P. M. ram *Switzerland* came down the river, and anchored, communicating with us. She returned up the river, again. Mortar vessels below, commenced about nine o'clock, and continued firing during the watch, three of the enemy's guns at the same time firing inland upon our army in rear of Port Hudson, and continuing their firing until a late hour; at eleven P. M. quick discharges of musketry heard in rear of Port Hudson, and two rockets seen sent up from that vicinity. It is reported as being true, that Banks has lost, up to the present time, from his late engagements with the enemy, some two thousand men in killed and wounded. Of one negro regiment, numbering a thousand men, when they charged the rebel works on the morning of the 27th of May last, six hundred remain to tell the fate of their comrades. This speaks well for their bravery.

June 4th. Commences with pleasant and calm weather. Slight firing heard, early this morning, at Port Hudson. Nothing worthy of mention occurred during the remainder of this day.

June 5th. Slight firing heard at Port Hudson, from twelve, midnight, until two o'clock A. M.; at four A. M. firing again heard at Port Hudson. Nothing of importance occurred during the remainder of this day, although our army in the rear of and fleet below

Port Hudson, engaged with the enemy. Having the range of their batteries, our forces, army and naval, have made some splendid shots this day, hitting their target and plowing up the earth around every time. Our mortar schooners must be a source of great annoyance to the enemy, both night and day, since they are continually at work practicing upon their mark, and seldom fail in hitting same, or coming so near to it, that it can be anything but agreeable to the parties who have to stand and take it, and are holding out so long at Port Hudson, I mean the rebs. They pass many sleepless nights, I can assure you, with these missiles of destruction, the shell of the bombers, flying over their heads, sometimes exploding in the air, other times on *terra firma*, close at their feet.

June 6th. Early this morning the shell from the mortar vessels was seen exploding over the rebel batteries; at ten A. M. our Assistant Surgeon, S. D. Kennedy, being detached, left the ship for New Orleans, for passage North. Artillery firing was heard in rear of Port Hudson during the remainder of this day.

June 7th. Slight firing from pieces of artillery, heard in rear of Port Hudson, early this morning; at ten A. M. ship and crew inspected by Commodore; at ten thirty, called all hands to muster, performed Divine service, and mustered crew around capstan. Nothing more, worthy of being recorded, occurred during this day. I forgot here to mention, as is the custom in the naval service, on the first Sunday of every month, that the articles of war were read to the ship's company assembled together on the quarterdeck, before Divine service was performed, by the first Lieutenant and Executive Officer, Mr. L. A. Kimberly.

June 8th. At one thirty A. M., mortar vessels below opened fire upon the batteries; at nine A. M., inspected crew at quarters. Artillery firing heard in rear of Port Hudson. From eight P. M. to twelve midnight, firing of great guns heard, at Port Hudson.

June 9th. Commences with calm and warm weather. Mortar vessels bombarding batteries at Port Hudson from one thirty to four A. M. Between the hours of ten and twelve o'clock M., a cavalry detachment made a reconnoissance to left bank of land. The bombardment of Port Hudson by our army and navy continued, with slight intervals, during the whole of this day.

June 10th. Commenced with pleasant but warm weather. Thin clothing is the order of the day. At a little before daylight, the mortar vessels of lower fleet, engaging the rebel batteries; at nine A. M., inspected crew at quarters; at about this hour, great guns were fired in and in the rear of Port Hudson. During the watch from eight P. M. to midnight, the mortars inland, of the army, shelling the rebel works.

June 11th. Commenced with pleasant weather, wind from the S. W.; at three thirty A. M., a squall of wind came up, we having only one anchor down, the starboard one, thought proper to let the good old ship ride the gale out with two, so let go the port anchor; we had no sooner let it go, than we had to heave it up again, as the blow, or tornado, it seemed, coming on, was all over with. Mortar boats engaged bombarding Port Hudson batteries. Squally and rainy weather; at six P. M. raining very hard—clearing off between seven and eight o'clock—accompanied by fresh breezes from S. S. E. Firing at Port Hudson continued the whole of these twenty-four hours.

June 12th. At one thirty A. M., steamer *Laurel Hill* came down from Natchez, with despatches. Occasional artillery firing, also navy and army mortars bombarding the batteries of Port Hudson—rebels reply with a large rifle; at eight A. M., heavy musketry and artillery firing in rear of Port Hudson. Steamer *Bee*, despatch boat, came down from Bayou Sara; at eleven twenty P. M., the mortar vessels of lower fleet engaged the rebel batteries, and making some good shots.

June 13th. A fire was seen early this morning down by the lower fleet, also at the same time, heavy bombardment of Port Hudson going on, by our army and naval forces. Between the hours of four and eight A. M., heavy firing of musketry, artillery, &c., at Port Hudson; at nine A. M. inspected crew at quarters; at five

P. M. the *Albatross* came down the river and anchored ahead of us. Mortars of lower fleet still firing, and the rebels replying with their lower batteries; at ten o'clock P. M., our mortar schooners still at work in their attempt to reduce Port Hudson. Clear and pleasant weather the whole of the twenty-four hours.

June 14th. At ten A. M. inspected crew at quarters, and performed Divine service. Slight artillery and musketry-firing in the rear of Port Hudson. Slight northerly breezes. Bombardment of Port Hudson, by the army and navy, kept up throughout this day, with slight intermission.

June 15th. At 1 o'clock A. M. the mortars of the army and navy firing into Port Hudson; at two forty-five A. M. the mortars of lower fleet ceased bombardment. From this time up to four A. M. brisk firing of musketry—the rebels replying with two guns; at two thirty P. M. got up steam; at four P. M. hauled fires; at nine fifteen P. M. beat to quarters. Several transports came down from Bayou Sara, on account of guerillas being about.

June 16. Commences with pleasant weather, and the bombardment of Port Hudson still going on—enemy not deigning to make any reply; at ten A. M. received some fresh beef on board from shore, for ship's company. Gunboat *Estrella*, and steamers *Louisiana Belle* and *Bee*, got under way and started up the river—destination, Bayou Sara. Saw a fire in the vicinity of the upper batteries at Port Hudson. Steamer *Bee* came down the river, during the afternoon, with despatches; at three P. M. heavy squalls of wind and rain. Between the hours of six and eight o'clock, received provisions from lower fleet, overland.

June 17th. Early this morning, mortars of lower fleet firing at intervals. At ten A. M. gunboat *Sachem* came down the river with despatches, and anchored ahead of the *Albatross*, off Falls river; burned several buildings on left bank of river; artillery and musketry firing in rear of Port Hudson, which continued until twelve o'clock; at ten thirty P. M., two rockets were seen sent up from Port Hudson.

June 18th. Bombardment of Port Hudson by our army and navy going on at an early hour this morning; at three forty-five P. M., the steamer *Arizona* came down the river. Nothing more worthy of mention occurred during the day.

June 19th. Commences with calm and pleasant weather. At nine A. M., inspected crew at quarters. Mr. Watson and Lieut. Eaton of U. S. A. signal Corps, went overland to lower fleet. From eight P. M. to midnight, occasional firing in rear of Port Hudson.

June 20th. Slight firing early this morning in rear of Port Hudson; at five A. M. the steamer *Bee* arrived from above Bayou Sara, having on board the pilot of gunboat *Lafayette*, who has come down as bearer of despatches to Commodore Palmer. At four twenty P. M., heavy artillery firing going on in rear of Port Hudson, showing that our army is not asleep, but on the other hand, harassing the enemy by day, while our mortar schooners and sloops-of-war of lower fleet harass him by night. I think by this plan of operations by the army and navy, the rebels cut off from obtaining supplies, will soon have to surrender to our forces.

June 21st. Commences with pleasant weather. From twelve to four A. M., heavy firing going on at Port Hudson, mostly of musketry. At ten A. M., inspected crew at quarters, and performed Divine service upon the quarter-deck. Between the hours of eight P. M. and twelve midnight, heard reports of great guns in rear of Port Hudson.

June 22d. Firing of musketry and artillery the whole forenoon of this day, in rear of Port Hudson. At nine P. M. steamer *Laurel Hill* arrived from Natchez.

June 23d. The forenoon of this day pleasant, but afternoon and evening squally and rainy. Firing at intervals heard at Port Hudson during the whole day.

June 24th. At seven thirty A. M. the steamer *Bee* came down the river with despatches. All quiet at Port Hudson.

June 25th. Early this morning, before daylight, slight firing of musketry and artillery commenced, and continued during nearly the whole day, at Port Hudson.

June 26th. This morning received on board two deserters from Port Hudson. They made their escape by swimming Thompson's creek, and report the rebel garrison living on half rations, and in expectancy of soon having to eat mule beef. If such be the case, Port Hudson must soon be surrendered to our forces. Many are deserting from there at present, and coming within our lines. From four to six P. M., firing going on at Port Hudson; from eight o'clock to midnight, moderate firing from mortars and guns of lower fleet upon the enemy's works.

June 27th. At seven thirty A. M., steamer *Bee* came down from Bayou Sara. Connonading going on at Port Hudson all this day.

June 28th. Commences with pleasant weather. Occasional firing at Port Hudson by the army mortars and great guns. At nine fifty A. M., inspected crew at quarters, and performed Divine service. Firing still going on at Port Hudson. This afternoon despatches were sent by Paymaster Meredith to Gen. Banks's headquarters. At one P. M. an orderly came on board from the General's headquarters. Steamer *Bee* came down the river, from Bayou Sara, with despatches and three soldiers of the 75th regiment N. Y. V., who were arrested at St. Francisville. From eight o'clock to twelve midnight, artillery firing heard in the rear of Port Hudson.

June 29th. From twelve midnight to four o'clock this morning the mortars and batteries of the army firing from the rear into the rebel batteries, the enemy not taking any notice whatever. This morning, Lieut. J. H. Higbee, U. S. M. C., with a corporal, went over to the army in charge of the three prisoners of the 75th regiment of N. Y. V. At nine o'clock, inspected crew at quarters. The bombardment of Port Hudson, or Gibraltar No. 2 on the Mississippi, still going on, and continued through the remainder of this day.

June 30th. At eight in the morning the steamer *St. Maurice* came down the river with a load of contrabands,—men, women and children,—which she got off of some plantation near Red river. Brisk artillery and musketry firing heard in rear of Port Hudson all this day. At three thirty in the afternoon received a mail on board from the lower fleet.

July 1st. Commences with clear and pleasant weather; at nine A. M., inspected crew at quarters; at ten thirty steamer *Estrella* came down the river and communicated with us; our naval battery below has been firing steadily all day, but the rebels did not reply.

July 2. Commences with pleasant but very warm weather; at nine A. M., inspected crew at quarters; from eleven A. M., until three P. M. firing of heavy guns heard in the rear of Port Hudson; the rebel water batteries firing at lower fleet.

July 3d. At seven A. M., sent some ammunition ashore to our naval battery; at ten thirty, Mr. Jas. B. Kimball, chief-engineer, left the ship, being detached and ordered North; at three P. M., steamer *Bee* came down from Bayou Sara and communicated with us. Firing in rear of Port Hudson still going on.

July 4th. This is the eighty-seventh anniversary of our national independence—a day dear to every true American heart on account of the event it commemorates; but since no salute has been fired by us in honor of the day, and Jack looks rather crest-fallen in the phiz on that account, still we have far more and greater reasons for being of the opposite cast of countenance than we had one year ago to-day. Let us look back into the past, as long ago as a twelvemonth since, and see what was our situation and condition then, and what our prospects of success in struggles about to take place for the supremacy of our arms. By reference to the author's remarks of what occurred on the Fourth of July, 1862, one year ago to-day, you will please note the fact that Vicksburg, although having withstood, about three weeks since, a terrific naval bombardment from our vessels, still defied our powers. Now the tables are turned; General Grant, in command of U. S. forces, has invested the place and cut off supplies reaching same for the rebel army by railroad from Jackson, Miss., and a surrender of this rebel stronghold is looked for at an early day; in fact, I must say it was not Grant, even Unconditional Surrender Grant, or any other general, who has been mainly instrumental in bringing about this condition of things, although he has performed, as I have before stated, no mean part in the programme of action, but this ship, under the superintendence of Admiral Farragut, by taking the lead of the fleet in the experiment of running the rebel batteries of Port Hudson, on the ever-to-be-remembered night of the 14th March last, and by the mercy of Almighty God, being fortunate enough to pass safely through that fiery ordeal with so little loss of life, with a gunboat (tender) lashed to her port side; also a few days afterwards, another battery of the enemy at Grand Gulf on our way up the river to Warrenton, to have communication with Major-General Grant and Acting Rear Admiral Porter, and again on our return, permitted to repass the above-mentioned battery at Grand Gulf with little loss of life and injury to ship, arriving off the mouth of Red river, which it had been previously decided upon we should blockade for the purpose of cutting off supplies from being transported by rebel steamers out of this stream to the rebel army at Port Hudson and Vicksburg, and aiding General Banks with his forces coming round from New Orleans by way of Berwick's Bay. Alexandria, and Atchafalaya river to get in rear of Port Hudson. While Admiral Farragut has rigidly enforced the blackade of the mouth of Red river, commenced by him with but two vessels, the *Hartford* and *Albatross* soon after the passage of the rebel fortifications at Port Hudson, cutting off relief from Texas reaching them by transportation down and out of this channel, or that of their fellows at Port Hudson, and starvation is now staring them in the face, making and early surrender of both places highly probable.

July 5th. At ten A. M., ship and crew inspected by the Commodore. Performed Divine service on the quarter-deck. Occasional firing at Port Hudson all this day.

July 6th. At nine in the morning inspected crew at quarters. Ship's company engaged in repairing fore and main standing-rigging, which has been shot away in action. Between the hours of four and six in the afternoon, U. S. naval batteries were engaged with the enemy at Port Hudson. From eight o'clock till twelve midnight, heavy squalls of wind and rain, accompanied with thunder and lightning. All quiet at Port Hudson at this hour.

July 7th. The miniature army steamer *Bee* (General Banks's despatch boat,) came down from Bayou Sara, at 12 o'clock midnight, bringing the cheering news of the fall of Vicksburg, which she had previously received from the steamer *Gen. Sterling Price,* just arrived from Vicksburg, and now lying aground off Point Coupée, opposite Bayou Sara. General Pemberton of the C. S. A., in command of the forces at Vicksburg, surrendered that city to General U. S. Grant (or, as he is more familiarly known, "Unconditional Surrender Grant"), in command of the Union forces, at ten o'clock on the morning of the glorious Fourth of July. An armistice between both armies had taken place on the evening previous. At eight A. M., steamers *Gen. Price* and *Empire Parish* came down the river—the former with despatches and a mail for us. Lieutenant Watson started for General Banks's headquarters, and Ensign Hazeltine for the lower fleet, with the news of the surrender of Vicksburg. From twelve noon until one thirty P. M., heavy cannonading at Port Hudson, on the left and right wings of the army; between the hours of five and six o'clock, the steamer *General Price,* with our mail on board, left for Vicksburg.

July 8th. At eight o'clock in the morning an orderly from General Banks's headquarters came on board, bringing despatches for the Commodore. Very soon after he had left the ship we started fires and got up steam, as did also all the gunboats and army transports around us. Between the hours of four and six P. M., heavy squalls of wind and rain came up from the northward and westward, accompanied with thunder and lightning. At six thirty, received the news of General Gardner, C. S. A. at Port Hudson, having surrendered to Major-General Banks, U. S. A., "in rear of same." The event occurred at two o'clock of this day, and was received with great joy. From six to eight o'clock, the army forces at Port Hudson signalized to us, we answering their signals.

July 9th. At one A. M., received despatches from General Banks, and half an hour afterwards ordered the transports to get under way and report at Mount Pleasant Landing. Colonel Smith came on board, a bearer of despatches form General Banks, with orders to report for passage to Vicksburg. At three thirty A. M. the transports went down the river; at four thirty our Paymaster went below, in steamer *Bee*, for stores; at eight thirty called all to up anchor, and never before, during the *Hartford's* cruise, was the anchor hove up by the boys with such a will and light hearts, or in a shorter period. The reader may here ask what was the stimulant administered to produce all this? In a few words I will tell him. The lads had been made to believe that the ship had been ordered home, and would leave New Orleans for the North very soon after she should arrive at that point, and general liberty had been given them; also there was another thing which made them light at heart: it was, that Port Hudson and Vicksburg had fallen, leaving the Mississippi clear from the Gulf to Cincinnati and St. Louis, and they had been in part instrumental in bringing about this work and felt proud of it. At nine A. M., came to anchor above Port Hudson batteries on account of some part of our machinery getting heated; at ten o'clock got under way again and stood down past Port Hudson; at ten ten the army firing a salute when the American flag was raised over the place; at ten forty-five came to anchor below Port Hudson; the gunboat *Albatross* accompanied us down; made signal to *Richmond* and *New London* at anchor here; finished taking provisions from steamer *Bee* on board during the afternoon; at seven thirty P. M., the steamer *Laurel Hill* passed down loaded with troops; at ten o'clock the transports *St. Maurice*, *Empire Parish*, *Union*, *St. Charles*, *General Banks*, and *Louisiana Bell* passed down the river with troops.

July 10th. At six o'clock this morning we hove up anchor, got under way, and steamed up to the batteries at Port Hudson, the *Albatross* in company with us. Came to anchor off same; hove up anchor and shifted our berth on account of eddies; some of our officers left the ship to visit the place which had lately gained so much notoriety; at eleven thirty Major-General Banks visited the ship, and at twelve forty-five left same to go ashore; the blue jackets manned the rigging and gave him three cheers, which he acknowledged by uncovering his head and politely bowing; at one o'clock got under way again and started down the river. When a short distance below Port Hudson passed and spoke the gunboat *Winona* coming up; she stated that she had despatches from the Admiral for Commodore Palmer and Capt. Jenkins of the U. S. steam sloop-of-war *Richmond.* We told her to come within hail, but since she did not seem to hear us, still keeping on her course, we sent the *Albatross* up after her to get the despatches for first-named party. We continued on our way down the Mississippi; at five thirty came to anchor off Baton Rouge.

July 11th. Commences with light winds from the westward; at four forty-five A. M. got under way and steamed down the river; at nine ten went to general quarters; at nine thirty anchored off Donaldsonville; at ten fifty went to general quarters once more, and prepared for action; fired the forward Parrott rifle at the different points as we passed; fired the broadside guns at embrasures cut in the levee from which our vessels lately were fired upon by pieces of rebel flying artillery, but received no response; steaming down the river in charge of pilot; passed between the hours of twelve and four P. M., the sloop-of-war *Monongahela* and iron-clad *Essex,* gunboat, at anchor; the lads manned the rigging and cheered ship, which was vociferously returned by them; the steamers *Albatross* and *Estrella* were in company with us; about five P. M., passed the U. S. sloop-of-war *Portsmouth* anchored off Carrollton; from her we received another cheer which we quickly returned; she also dipped her colors as we were passing; cheer upon cheer rent the air from youngsters and grown-up persons on shore, who had seen us approaching, and flocked down to the levee to give expression to their feelings of joy at seeing the noble old ship *Hartford* once more, which they had begun to have a sort of veneration for on account of the great deeds she had performed, making her name to be held in dread by all traitors to their country; about six thirty passed the *Pensacola,* rounded to and at six thirty-five had ship cheered by *Pensacola* and *Tennessee,* which we returned; at six forty came to anchor off the city of New Orleans. Soon the news spread of our arrival, and crowds of people flocked down to the levee to see us once more; they were informed by those in sympathy with the rebels, (loyal now because they were forced to be to save their property from confiscation, and themselves from being sent beyond our lines), that in attempting to pass the batteries at Port Hudson on the 14th of March last we had been sunk, and they, in proof of the truth of their statement, referred to the fact that when the *Hartford* left New Orleans last, she was painted black, and the vessel before them was of a light lead color; in fact they so talked their theory into them that they believe it to be the truth; even the statement of the *Era*, a daily loyal sheet, that the *Hartford* had arrivd, was not believed, and some of our boys ashore on liberty, with the ship's name on their hats, could not make them believe any different; in fact, they could not be made to believe it until parties had been on board who were acquainted with some of our officers, and returned, having seen them, and learned we had the power of changing our plumage wherever we might be.

July 12th. At anchor off New Orleans. Between the hours of four and eight o'clock this morning, the gunboat *Winona* arrived from up the river; at ten o'clock inspected crew at quarters, also performed Divine service. This afternoon, commenced giving liberty to our men, about fifty at a time.

July 13th. At one thirty A. M., the U. S. mail steamer *Creole* came up the river; at seven o'clock, U. S. mail steamer *George Cromwell*, arrived; at ten thirty, a heavy rain shower came up from the southward and westward which lasted about an hour. Carpenters were engaged repairing ship's side. The boatswain and crew engaged repairing rigging and getting ship ready for sea, for a homewardbound trip. Lieut. John C. Watson left the ship to go on board of Flag-ship *Tennessee*, and report for duty to the Admiral, having been temporarily detached from the *Hartford*.

July 14th. Commences with clear and pleasant weather. Engaged during the whole 24 hours, coaling ship; at one P. M., gave liberty to 2nd Division, twenty-four hours; at two, the steamer *Zephyr* came down the river; at five the *Albatross* went down the river.

July 15th. At seven forty-five A. M., the U. S. mail steamship *Columbia* arrived from New York, bringing mails and passengers. This afternoon, broke down the cotton bales around poop, and sent them ashore (sixteen bales), since we needed them for a barricade no longer, our fighting days being over; also employed coaling ship, repairing damages to rigging, &c; at five P. M. the U. S. steam sloop-of-war *Portsmouth* came down, in tow of a steam-tug; at six, finished coaling ship; at seven thirty, two river steamers arrived with rebel prisoners from above, Vicksburg and Port Hudson.

July 16th. Commenced with pleasant and calm weather, as usual. Crew at quarters at nine A. M., and loosed sail to day. Took the fish off the mizzen-mast, and got topsail-yard ready for sending aloft; at eleven forty-five, furled sail, and during the remainder of this day, employed in repairing rigging, and fishing mizzen-mast.

July 17th. Calm and pleasant. Carpenter's gang employed during the day fishing mizzen-mast, and crew at work repairing rigging, fore and aft.

July 18th. At eight A. M., U. S. M. steamer *George Cromwell* sailed for New York, with mails and passengers. Work going on this day, viz: repairing rigging, fishing mizzen mast, and provisioning ship, &c.

July 19th. At seven A. M., steamer *Albatross* came up the river, with the gunboat *Sciota* in tow, the latter being out of repair; at nine thirty this morning, inspected crew and ship, and at ten, called all hands to muster on quarterdeck, where Divine services were performed, Commodore Palmer's clerk, Nathaniel P. S. Thomas, officiating. Read General Order No. 16, from Navy Department, Washington, D. C., upon the death of Rear-Admiral Foote, who died at the Astor House, N. Y., lately, surrounded by his numerous friends and associates, who deeply deplore his loss. He had been ordered to relieve Admiral Dupont, in command of the South Atlantic Blockading Squadron, off Charleston, and was on his way to perform that duty, when he was taken sick in the city of New York, and as I have stated, death ensued. This afternoon, gunboat *Estrella* went down the river, and the *Arizona* arrived from Vicksburg.

July 20th. Early this morning, a side-wheel steamer came up the river. Hoisted two rifle guns off the poop, and transported them forward. Some of the lads on liberty; those remaining on board, some of whom had been ashore and had a little run of it, working with a will, since they were now sure that the old and loved *Hartford* was homeward bound. The guns, eight in number, had been ordered to be got in readiness for being hoisted out of her, which was a sure indication that they were quite right in believing as they did. During the forenoon, sent two guns and carriages ashore; at three P. M. gunboat *Estrella* got under way and went down the river; at six forty, inspected crew at evening quarters, and transported two guns from the starboard to port side of deck. This was a good day's work done, darkness coming on before the boys got through with it.

July 21st. Between the hours of four and six A. M., slight fog. During the remainder of the forenoon, employed getting ammunition and guns ready to send on shore. During the afternoon, sent third cutter on shore for repairs; also sent two nine-inch Dahlgren guns and equipments, and a quantity of grape.

July 22d. Between the hours of four and eight A. M. steamer *Crescent City* came down the river with troops—some of Banks's army. During the remainder of this day got ready, hoisted into launch, and sent one nine-inch Dahlgren and one thirty pounder Parrott rifle on shore; at six P. M. steamer *Tennessee* got under way and steamed down the river, with Admiral Farragut on board. Weather pleasant, but very warm.

July 23d. At six o'clock this morning, steamer *Eugenie* came up and anchored ahead of us, having our top-gallant and royal masts, also yards and rigging on board, which she had been to Pensacola for; at nine inspected crew at quarters; at nine thirty, sent our launch to steamer *Eugenie*, and brought on board our spars. Engaged repairing rigging during the afternoon or remainder of this day—got main top-gallant and royal yards in the rigging and painted them, and employed in sending aloft top-gallant rigging and getting top-gallant masts ready to send aloft. Weather cool and pleasant. Men very busy.

July 24th. During the morning received fresh beef and vegetables for crew. Carpenters at work repairing fore-top-gallant mast; at two P. M. had top-gallant mast ready to send aloft.

July 25th. During forenoon of this day, engaged in fitting top-gallant and royal yards. Bent fore and main top-gallant sails and royals, and placed them in the rigging; also bent the foresail and mizzen topsail. Gunboat *New London* went down the river. During the hours of eight and ten P. M., squalls of rain accompanied by thunder and lightning; wind from the southward.

July 26th. At ten P. M., inspection of ship and crew by Commodore Palmer; at ten thirty called all hands to muster, and performed Divine service on the quarter-deck; at five thirty in the afternoon steamer *Lancaster* came down the river with a load of rebel prisoners.

July 27th. At three A. M. the sloop-of-war *Seminole* came up and anchored astern of the *Portsmouth*; at six o'clock, the U. S. gunboat *Genesee* arrived from up the river; at 9 o'clock, as usual, inspected crew at quarters. During the remainder of this day, engaged setting up topmast-rigging. At five P. M., steamer *General Banks* went down the river with rebel prisoners, under a flag of truce, for Mobile.

July 28th. Commences with pleasant weather and light westerly winds. The following is what has transpired this day:—At eight A. M. the U. S. steamer *Virginia* arrived; at three P. M. the *Monongahela* came down the river and anchored off the *Richmond's* starboard quarter. Ship's company engaged getting ship ready for sea.

July 29th. At two thirty A. M. a propeller came up the river, and at two forty the gunboat *Katahdin.* The latter anchored off our starboard bow. At six o'clock sent fourth cutter to *Tennessee*, and brought off spare main and topsail yard, and sent up a new one; stowed outboard damaged main topsail yard; painted spare topsail yard. At ten P. M. the steamer *Westmoreland* arrived from Vicksburg, with two days later news from the North.

July 30th. At one thirty A. M. gunboat *Albatross* went down the river; at ten o'clock gunboat *Katahdin* got under way and steamed down the river; at one P. M. received on board some of Admiral Farragut's baggage. During the afternoon Mr. VanDenhougle, late Admiral Farragut's Secretary, reported on board for passage to New York. Sent aloft topmast and topgallant studding sail booms; at four thirty P. M. U. S. steam sloop-of-war *Richmond* got under way, turned around, and went down the river. As she passed, our lads manned the rigging and gave them three hearty farewell cheers, which they returned. We were well aware our day for following in her path homeward-bound was now near at hand, and she was the messenger sent to announce our coming. The reader need not be informed of the feelings of all on board the *Hartford*, since he knows all must have been in high spirits.

July 31st. At nine A. M. inspected crew at quarters. Fleet-Surgeon J. M. Foltz reported on board for passage home. During the afternoon Commodore Morris, late of U. S. steam sloop *Pensacola* was hoisted inboard, upon a cot, an invalid, for passage to the North.

August 1st. Commences with pleasant weather. At nine thirty A. M. the U. S. gunboat *Black Hawk*, with Admiral D. D. Porter on board, came down the river, accompanied by the gunboat *Conestoga*. As they passed they fired a salute of fourteen guns, which the U. S. S. *Portsmouth* returned, and we cheered ship. Admiral Porter visited the ship, and was received by the marine guard. At six thirty P. M. called all hands up anchor, got under way and steamed up the river and turned round. Was cheered as we passed the fleet, which we returned. The church bells in the city also were rung. Stood down the river in charge of pilot.

August 2d. Steaming down the river; at two ten o'clock in the morning a shot fired across our bow from Fort St. Philip, to heave us to; stopped the ship, and was boarded by an officer; at two fifteen started ahead again; at three forty S. W. Pass light in sight; at six thirty A. M. crossed the bar, and pilot left the ship; at nine o'clock made a sail off the starboard bow, bore down to her and spoke her. She proved to be the U. S. mail steamer *Locust Point*, from New York, bound for New Orleans. At ten o'clock ship and crew inspected by the Commodore, after which performed Divine service on the quarter-deck.

August 3d. At sea; at eleven in the morning light rain squall passed over; at eleven thirty set all fore and aft sails; at eleven forty-five took them in; at three fifteen P. M. light rain-squall passed over; at four ten made a sail to the southward, and bore down for her, called all hands make sail, and at four thirty fired a gun in direction of strange sail, which hoisted the French colors. Furled sail and hauled up to course again. Unbent and sent down foretopsail for repairs, and sent up and bent a new one. At six ten inspected crew at quarters. From eight o'clock to midnight slight wind from southward and eastward, and clear; at eleven fifty a sail reported on starboard beam.

August 4th. At twelve midnight stood off to west-southwest in chase of a sail; at twelve fifteen A. M. discovered her to be a brig, standing to northward and eastward, closehauled; stood on our course again; braced yards up by port braces, and then again by starboard braces; at three fifteen set mizzen-topmast stay-sail, and at three thirty fore-topmast stay-sail, jib, and main trysail; also set the spanker; at five o'clock hoisted our colors to an American barque standing to northward and westward.

August 5th. At twelve thirty A. M. took in all fore and aft sails; at five thirty braced around the yards; made a sail off port quarter, and one off port beam; at eight forty made Tortugas light house, bearing, per compass, northeast; at five thirty P. M. Sand Key light reported two points on port bow; at six thirty made Key West light off port bow—strong breezes from the eastward; at eight fifteen spoke ship *Mayflower*, from New York, bound to New Orleans; at eleven o'clock made Sombrero light.

August 6th. At nine A. M. made all sail; sent aloft the royals and set them; practiced ship's company at general quarters, without powder; made Cape Florida light; four sails reported in sight during watch; saw a large steamer standing to the southward.

Aug. 7th. Commences, and until four A. M. pleasant weather; from four o'clock to eight o'clock braced sharp up on port tack; all plain sail set to royals; made a sail off starboard bow, and one off starboard beam; from twelve to four P. M. exercised the fore and main royal yardsmen in furling and loosening royals; at two o'clock set the foretop-gallant and topmast studding sails; at three o'clock took them in; passed a brig bound the same course; at six thirty laid the yards square, and took in all fore and aft sails except the jib; braced sharp upon starboard tack, and set foretop-gallant studding sails; at six forty-five inspected crew at evening quarters; from eight to midnight all plain sail set to royals.

Aug. 8th. Commences with pleasant weather; hauled down and shifted over starboard foretop-gallant studding sails, set the foretop-gallant and topmast studding sails, hauled down jib and flying jib, brailed up the main topmast stay-sail and main try-sail; at three thirty set the main fore topmast stay-sail main try-sail and spanker, bending lower studding sails; from four o'clock to eight o'clock set the port lower studding sails, jib and flying jib; at nine o'clock inspected crew at quarters; all plain sail set to royals, also all port studding sails; exercised crew at taking in, loosening, furling, and setting royals and mizzen top-gallant sails; from four to six P. M., all plain sail set to royals, and all the port fore studding sails set also; at seven thirty made Hatteras light.

Aug. 9th. At twelve forty-five A. M., a light reported off port-quarter; at two o'clock took in and furled all the studding and square sails; at six o'clock set all plain sail to royals; at six thirty made a sail off weather bow, proved to be a schooner, standing on same course; weather clear and pleasant; at nine o'clock made a sail off port bow, and at twelve, noon, one right ahead; had inspection at quarters, and performed Divine service; at two P. M., passed a steamer standing to the southward, also passed the *John Adams* who made her number, which we answered; several sail in sight; at four thirty set all the port studding sails; clear and pleasant; at sundown three sail were in sight.

Aug. 10th. At twelve thirty A. M., passed a brig standing to the northward and eastward; at two thirty trimmed sails to the wind; set port fore-topmast and top-gallant studding sails; got port lower studding sails ready for setting; took in studding sails, and braced yards up to shift of wind; at three o'clock Delaware light-boat bore, per compass, north by west; at seven thirty Barnegat lighthouse reported; at nine o'clock, stood up for a pilot boat; at nine forty-five took a pilot on board; several sail in sight during watch; at eleven o'clock set the jib, flying jib, and main topmast stay-sail; at twelve o'clock set the main try-sail; at two P. M., steamer *Golden Gate* met and cheered us, which we returned; at three o'clock crossed the bar, at which time the battery on Sandy Hook saluted us with fifteen guns, returned with thirteen; sent down royal and squared yards; from four to six o'clock steaming up New York harbor; received salutes from the lower fleet, also Forts Hamilton and the Battery, which we returned; received a salute from an English sloop-of-war, and from a Spanish frigate, which we answered; at five thirty rounded to, and anchored off the Battery.

ADDENDA

LIST OF KILLED AND WOUNDED.

April 24th, 1862.

Joseph Lawrence, seaman, killed; Wm. H. Brown, landsman, killed; Augustus Thomas, captain forecastle (April 25th), wounded; Philip Morgan, seaman, severely wounded; Chas. H. Banks (colored), landsman, severely wounded; Theo. Douglass (colored), officers' steward, severely wounded; Randall Talliaferro, (cont'd,) landsman, thigh amputated; Henry Manning, O. S., (colored,) severely wounded; Henry King, marine, severely wounded; Zebina L. Doane, seaman, slightly wounded; George White, marine, slightly wounded; Jas. H. Conley, carpenter, severely wounded; Geo. Heisler, U. S. M. C., slightly wounded.—Total, 10.

June 28th, 1862

Edward E. Jennings, seaman, killed; Flag-Officer, D. G. Farragut wounded (slight contusion); Capt. Jno. L. Broome, U. S. Marine Corps, contusion; Chas. Allen seaman, slightly wounded; Philip Roberts, seaman, severely wounded; Jno. H. Knowles, Quartermaster, slightly wounded; Joseph Garido, O. S., slightly wounded; Nathan J. Salter, O. S., contusion; Alfred Stone, Landsman, slightly wounded; Sylvester Backus (colored), landsman; Lawrence Fay, boy, slightly wounded; Patrick Roach, coal heaver, head; Alex'r Caper (colored), landsman, slightly wounded; John Hartigan, landsman, slightly wounded.—Total, 13.

July 15th, 1862—Vicksburg.

Geo. H. Lounsberry, master's mate, killed; John H. Cameron, seaman, killed; Chas. Jackson, officers' cook, killed; Capt. Jno.

L. Broome, Marine Corps, contusion of head and shoulder; Thos. Hoffman, Paymaster's steward, struck in the head and chest with splinters; Jno. D. Barnes, fireman, contusion of shoulder; Geo. B. Royer, marine, slight contusion of arm; Michael Martin, landsman, slight contusion of arm; Henry Downes (colored), boy, slight contusion of arm.

MARCH 19TH, 1863.—GRAND GULF

Charles Sweeney, landsman, killed; Dennis Driscoll, landsman, killed; Wm. Brown, seaman, slightly wounded.

MARCH 31ST, 1863.—GRAND GULF.

Wm. Jones, landsman, killed; Wm. Brown, seaman, severely wounded.

MARCH 4TH, 1863.—PORT HUDSON.

Thos. F. Butler, marine, killed; Fred'k F. Carr, Captain F. C. slightly wounded; Daniel McCarthy, seaman, slightly wounded in head.

Zeitfracht Medien GmbH
Ferdinand-Jühlke-Straße 7
99095 Erfurt, Deutschland
produktsicherheit@kolibri360.de